Landscape Design
@Asia Pacific

george lam / pace publishing ltd

© 2008 by Pace Publishing Limited

editor : george lam (george.lam@beisistudio.com)
design + colour edit : polly leung

pace publishing limited
17/f., north point asia-pac commercial ctr.,
10 north point road,
hong kong
t: +852 28971688
f: +852 28972888
www.beisistudio.com
pace@pacebase.com

While all reasonable efforts have been made to ensure accuracy, Pace Publishing Limited and the publishers do not, under any circumstances, accept responsibility for errors, omissions and representations expressed or implied.
All rights reserved. No portion of "Landscape Design@Asia Pacific" may be reproduced or transmitted in any form or by any means electronic or mechanical, including photocopying, recording, or any information storage or retrieval system, without prior permission in writing from the publishers.

isbn 978-962-7723-86-8
printed in china

Institutional and Commercial

58~61	**The British Embassy, Sana'a, Yemen** Coe Design Landscape Architecture
62~65	**Whitireia Polytechnic, Porirua** Wraight + Associates Ltd.
66~69	**Deakin Central Precinct, Melbourne** Rush Wright Associates
70~75	**Circle on Cavill, Gold Coast** Place Design Group
76~81	**Gate City Osaki, Tokyo** Thomas Balsley Associates
82~85	**Spy Valley, Marlborough** Wraight + Associates Ltd.
86~89	**Osaka World Trade Center** Thomas Balsley Associates
90~93	**Jimbocho City, Tokyo** Thomas Balsley Associates
94~97	**Mount Gambier Civic Buildings Heritage Precinct, South Australia** Fifth Creek Studio
98~101	**TarraWarra Estate, Victoria** Tract Consultants Pty Ltd.
102~109	**Pacific Harbour Golf & Country Club, Queensland** Place Design Group
110~115	**Radisson Resort Fiji, Nadi** Place Design Group
116~121	**Putrajaya Shangri La** ICN Design International
122~125	**Chiva Som International Spa at Khao Kho, Petchaboon** Coe Design Landscape Architecture

Parks and Gardens

128~135	**Genesis Masterplanned Community, Queensland** Place Design Group
136~141	**Royal Park Wetlands, Melbourne** Rush Wright Associates
142~147	**Kota Kemuning Wetland Park, Shah Alam** ICN Design International
148~153	**Wetland 5, Sydney Park, Sydney** ASPECT Studios Pty Ltd.

154~157	**Ecology Park, Cibinong Science Centre, West Java** Sheils Flynn Ltd.
158~163	**Former BP Park, Waverton, Sydney** mcgregor+partners
164~167	**Twelve Apostles Visitors Centre, Victoria** Tract Consultants Pty Ltd.
168~173	**South East Asian Rainforest Immersion - The Adelaide Zoo** HASSELL
174~177	**Lory Loft at Jurong Birdpark, Singapore** Green & Dale Associates
178~183	**Waitangi Park, Wellington** Wraight Athfield Landscape + Architecture Ltd.
184~187	**Cairns Esplanade Skatepark, Queensland** Convic Design Pty Ltd.
188~191	**Belgrave Town Park, Victoria** ASPECT Studios Pty Ltd.
192~197	**Clewley Street Garden, Brisbane** Jeremy Ferrier Landscape Architects
198~201	**Habitat Wakerley, Brisbane** Jeremy Ferrier Landscape Architects

202~205	Manukau City Council Cultural Performance Garden 2006, Manurewa
Chow:Hill Architects Ltd.	246~255	**Company Profile**

206~209 Carnegie Library Play Space: The Bookworms, Victoria
FORMium / Mark McWha Landscape Architects

Residential

212~217 Glentrees Condominium, Singapore
ICN Design International

218~223 Southport Central, Queensland
Place Design Group

224~229 M Central, Sydney
360° Landscape Architecture

230~233 Vajra Villas, Ubud Bali
Sheils Flynn Ltd.

234~237 Tatham Residence, Queenstown
Morgan+Pollard Associates Queenstown

238~241 Edgar Landscape, Queenstown
Morgan+Pollard Associates Queenstown

242~245 Hocking Place Bushtop, Adelaide
Fifth Creek Studio

INTRODUCTION
Tom Turner

TOM TURNER teaches landscape architecture and garden history at the University of Greenwich, in London, and is the editor of the Gardenvisit.com website, which provides a Gardens Guide and a Landscape Architecture Guide. He is the author of English garden design since 1650 (1986), City as landscape – a post-Postmodern approach to design and planning (1995), Landscape planning and environmental impact design (1998), Garden history, philosophy and design 2000 BC – 2000 AD (2005). Currently, he is writing a book on the influence of religion on garden design in Asia.

Asia has a long tradition of designing gardens and landscapes. But their historical evolution was disrupted in the nineteenth century through contacts with Europe. Settlers made European-style houses and gardens for themselves, which came to influence Asian designers. In the twentieth century, Asia came progressively under the influence of International Modernism. Designs came to be based on reason and science, instead of beliefs and traditions. This presented an opportunity and a problem. The opportunity was to shake off the heavy hand of history. The problem was that designs became everywhere the same - because reason and science are everywhere the same.

Wherever you are in the world, 2+2=4, water flows downhill and concrete beams require reinforcement. People do not object to mobile phones and cars being everywhere the same, but I have asked many audiences if they would like gardens, landscapes and cities to be everywhere the same and the usual response is a disgusted 'Of course not!'.

I therefore invite readers of this book to consider the following questions when looking at the excellent designs and photographs in this book: 'Without looking at the text, can you tell which countries the design projects are located in?' When the answer is 'Yes', and you are correct, please move on to the following questions: 'How did you know?' 'Was the evidence based on the style of the architecture, the style of the landscape architecture or on previous knowledge of the design or its location?' People who know the region better than I do probably achieved a higher score, but for 90% of the projects my own answer was 'I haven't a clue'.

Assuming others will also find it difficult to locate the projects, we should then ask: 'does it matter?'. This question may receive different answers from professionals and from the public. The professionals, still in awe of International Modernism, tend to argue that we now live in one world which should be based on one set of principles. Politicians, voters and tourists tend to prefer diversity. But on what principles could context-sensitive landscape design be based?

The author of a famous book on Islamic architecture, Oleg Grabar, put the question as follows:

Thus we return to what I see as the fundamental question of our time: how can one preserve, in dignity, and with success, separate identities, when technology, ecology economics and the media all tend to homogenize their impact and their control? Should one even try?[1]

Grabar regretted what he saw as the probable demise of aesthetically identifiable Islamic architecture and we might also regret the demise of traditional Islamic, Chinese and Japanese gardens, except as historical relics and sentimental reconstructions. The problem is most acute in Australia, the country in which many of the projects in this book are located and in which pre-1788 architectural styles are unlikely to regain their popularity. Continuance of a British-colonial style of landscape or architectural design would seem equally inappropriate. Japan, also represented in this book, was the first Asia Pacific country to consider the issue of contextual design. Kenzo Tange wrestled with the issues in the 1930s and, in Hiroshima's Peace Park attempted a synthesis of East and West which, in my eyes, is far more West than East.

Context-sensitive Asian design could be based on a range of principles, including nationality, religion, ethnicity, geology, hydrology, sociology and ecology. In West Asia generally, and the Gulf states in particular, design in the second half of the twentieth century was firmly based on International Modernism. It was common for western consultants to recommend designs with 'local identity' and for their clients to want deigns which were fully 'up to date'. By the first decade of the twenty-first century, the tide was starting to change. Modern interpretations of Islamic forms, dhows and charhar bagh gardens are increasingly seen in resorts: it is what the tourists want and often the local residents as well.

The cultural questions await future resolution but, as a number of projects in this book indicate, the simplest and best approach to local identity is through the use of local plants and materials in landscape architecture. It is good for wildlife; it is sustainable; it can be very beautiful.

Taking a broad view of the subject, I reviewed the issues concerning context-sensitive design in Chapter 3 of and proposed the use of an Identity Index to summarize the relationship between a new project and its context:

In London's Isle of Dogs, there is hardly any visual similarity between the buildings, but conservation of the water bodies has created a spatial pattern which is similar to the pre-development landscape. A new reservoir in a beautiful place should be similar to other water bodies in the region. It was right to make the Sydney Opera House different from all surrounding buildings - and to give it a kinship with the sailing ships which pass by. These examples illustrate different Identity policies. Each has its place, but design teams should be required to explain the stance they have taken on the various aspects of identity between development and environment. Each contextual relationship requires the support of a coherent argument. Projects must be designed 'from the outside in' and 'from the inside out'. Use of an Identity Index need not be a factor in deciding for or against the Australian's application for a church and Eucalypt forest. It would merely define the background against which his justification of the proposed contextual relationship would have to be developed.[2]

---

[1] Grabar, O., 'The mission and its people' in *Architecture for Islamic Societies Today*. Academy Editions 1994) p.11

[2] Turner, T., Landscape planning and environmental impact design. UCL Press, 1998, p. 103. Also available online at http://www.gardenvisit.com/book/landscape_planning_and_environmental_impact_design:_from_eia_to_eid/chapter_3_context_sensitive_design_theory/sid_identity_index_context_theory

Plazas, Squares and Streetscapes

Tokyo Midtown
EDAW, Inc.

awards
2007 Overall Best in Class: Property Initiative and Design, MIPIM Asia Award;
2007 Best Mixed-Use Development, MIPIM Asia Award.

EDAW served as master landscape architects in conjunction with New York master plan architects Skidmore, Owings and Merrill, and Nikken Sekkei to develop the former site of the self-defense agency in Roppongi, Tokyo, one of the largest mixed-use projects undertaken in Tokyo to date.

Tokyo Midtown, a twenty-five acre, world-class mixed-use complex has become a landmark for Tokyo and the premiere address in Japan. This new development encompasses over six million square feet of office, residential, retail and hotel, along with major open spaces of parks, streetscapes and urban plazas.

Tokyo is a dense urban metropolitan area with a population exceeding 18 million and a city with limited accessible open space. In contrast, Tokyo Midtown has allocated over fifty percent of the site's land to the public realm, of which two-thirds of the open space is green parks and gardens. Traditionally, green space in Tokyo is a collection of gardens and sacred spaces: landscapes designed to be looked at rather than used. Tokyo Midtown was designed as a network of open spaces that establish a new typology in the Japanese urban landscape.

Tokyo Midtown breaks the vernacular of how open space is used in Japan and addresses the human scale by encouraging a multiplicity of choice. "To celebrate nature and hospitality; entertaining and showing respect for the guest" was the client's vision and this was met through the seamless, holistic integration of the of the site's amenities. It is how people should live in an urban setting all within the easy reach of home, shopping, office and dining.

The Grand Plaza showing the curving architecture of the skylights.

↓ The Grand Plaza showing the curving architecture of the skylights and straight lines overlaid onto the horizontal plane.
↘ Custom bamboo light fixtures, which are situated throughout the Grand Plaza and purposely positioned between bamboo planting.

↑ The Grand Plaza at night.
→ The open space of the park is reaching out and intersecting with the urban streetscape.
↓ The plaza unites a western paving approach with Japanese elements, with 'Wa', where every piece of paving has a 2:1 ratio much like the Tatami Mat.
↘ The Grand Plaza enhances the visitors' experience—you can walk under lush canopies and relax near water features.

↓ The braided pedestrian paths, bridges and walkways that weave between the garden spaces and cherry trees create tension between the elements.

↓↓ The meandering stream leading the way to the Design Site.

↙ An historic stream once traversed the site and is now reinterpreted as a contemporary, romanticized water feature..

↑   A view of the braided pathway system intersecting and creating simple geometry.
↗   Tokyo Midtown at night.
→   Illustrative Plan.
↘   Wave shape elements—'Planters' and 'Custom Benches'—are peeling away vertically from the horizontal design.
↓   The 'Great Lawn' enhancing the interconnectivity of the landscape and architectural elements.

client
Mitsui Fudosan Co., Ltd.
team at edaw (SAN FRANCISCO DESIGN STUDIO)
Steve Hanson, Principal in charge - Design Lead;
Todd Kohli, Senior Associate, Landscape Architect;
Joe Brown, CEO, Principal Advisor;
Aki Omi, Senior Associate, Landscape Designer
other key consultants
Master Architects: SOM (NYC);
Communication Arts, Inc. (Boulder, Colorado);
Fisher Marantz Stone (NYC, NY);
Buro Happold (NYC, NY);
Nikken Sekkei, Ltd. (Tokyo, Japan);
Kengo Kuma & Associates (Tokyo, Japan);
Sakakura Associates Architects & Engineers (Tokyo, Japan);
Jun Aoki and Associates (Tokyo, Japan);
Tadao Ando Architect & Associates (Osaka, Japan);
Construction Team: Takenaka Corporation and Taisei Corporation (Tokyo, Japan)
location
Urban Planning Group, 1-1 Nihonbashi Muromachi 2-Chome, Chuou-Ku, Tokyo, Japan
completion
2007
photography
EDAW/David Lloyd unless stated

NewQuay Public Realm, Melbourne
Tract Consultants Pty Ltd

In 1998, the Docklands Authority awarded MAB the right to develop the majority of the northern waterfront of Victoria Harbour, with the remainder of the precinct scheduled for a major theme park by others.

Tract Consultants were commissioned by MAB Corporation as Urban Designers/ Landscape Architects as part of the project team to prepare a development masterplan for the Business Park Precinct of the Melbourne Docklands.

A specific client requirement was the creation of an urban art precinct, manifested by "contemporary" design philosophy and a comprehensive integrated urban art overlay. Stage 1 & 2 of New Quay East, comprised 5 Residential Towers on podiums with a highly activated waterfront promenade, plazas, lanes, streets and major entry boulevard.

The initial stages of New Quay were intended primarily as mixed use, higher density residential, however, a unique "harbourside" sense of place, underpinned by a vibrant cosmopolitan Melbourne character was considered the all important theme to both "market" the development as a place of difference, whilst setting a benchmark at Docklands.

The Concept was the creation of a range of integrated flowing public spaces whilst extending the style and higher quality of CBD Melbourne, is also intended as a subtle departure, contributing to a point of difference – The Fourth Quarter of Melbourne.

New Quay, the first precinct completed at Docklands, demonstrates that intelligence, combined with innovation, the creation of high quality, memorable public spaces can be achieved within the commercial realty of private sector developments.

awards
2005, Australian Institute of Landscape Architecture (AILA) Award.

← NewQuay waterfront promenade.
↓ Aerial view of promenade.
↙ East plaza light.

← Aerial view of site with Melbourne CBD in background.
↑ Waterfront promenade festival.
↓ Precinct Masterplan.

client
MAB Docklands Pty Ltd
other key consultants
Architects: FKA/SJB Architects in Association;
Project Managers: Project Planning and Management;
Civil Engineers: Coomes Pty Ltd;
Civil/Structural: Robert Bird and Associates;
Lighting: Webb Lighting;
Soils Scientist: Robert Van de Graaf;
Horticultural/Soil Specs: Dr Peter May;
Irrigation: Michael Tenburin;
Wind Assessment: Vipac;
Cost Control: Davis Langdon.
location
Melbourne CBD, Australia
completion
Ongoing
photography
Gollings

Taranaki Wharf, Wellington

**Wraight + Associates Ltd
with Athfield Architects Ltd**

Wellington is a compact city dominated by its striking landscape; an expansive harbour cradled by a commanding hilly terrain that accommodates an eclectic profusion of suburbia and urbania. In line with the global re-awakening of urban waterfronts, Wellington City has been quick to revitalise its once port-dominated harbour and capitalise on its distinctive character and proximity to the urban centre.

The principal elements of this design establish a critical public space on the knuckle of Lambton Harbour, directly connecting the city's urban business district with the harbour. The site comprises a necklace of flexible open spaces supported by a framework of generous promenades and bridge connections that take advantage of this unique harbour-city location. A variety of experiences have been consciously woven into the scheme from the intimate experience of the sheltered lagoon to the bracing exposure of the open harbour. Historical markings, artworks and introduced pockets of endemic ecologies permeate the scheme reflecting the site's cultural and natural heritage. The Lagoon, a sheltered intimate zone, accommodates a series of connections from the city's Civic Square to Te Papa Tongarewa (The Museum of New Zealand) and out to the wide exposed harbour promenade. A divided bridge provides an elevated experience over the lagoon entrance, connecting two halves of harbourside promenade. Treasure Island curls around the lagoon's rim supporting a myriad of pathways, intimate spaces and endemic coastal vegetation. It provides a definitive green picturesque armature to the Victorian rowing club buildings nestled between the lagoon and harbour's edge. A wide promenade circumnavigates the harbour edge; simple robust materials dominate with finer details reserved for places of transition and periphery. The promenade accommodates a number of engaging interventions: a dense grove of Karaka Trees – within which a sense of harbour is at once transposed by the closeness of an almost forest experience; The Cut-Out – offers a unique 'under wharf' experience where visitors are drawn down to water level amongst a forest of wharf piles, filtered light and dazzling light reflections; and the Linkspan and Bridge – retains the working harbour heritage of the site with a dry-dock with small drawbridge.

awards
*2004, George Malcolm Supreme Award, New Zealand Institute of Landscape Architects;
2006, Merit Award, International Federation of Landscape Architects.*

→ View over Taranki wharf to oversee passanger terminal.

← Timber Garden.
↖ Paving detail, wharf structure.
↖ Treasure Island 'writers walk' detail.
↑ Treasure Island.
↗ Taranaki Wharf bridge.
↗↗ Taranaki Wharf plan.
→ Looking east over lagoon towards Taranaki Wharf bridge and boatshed.

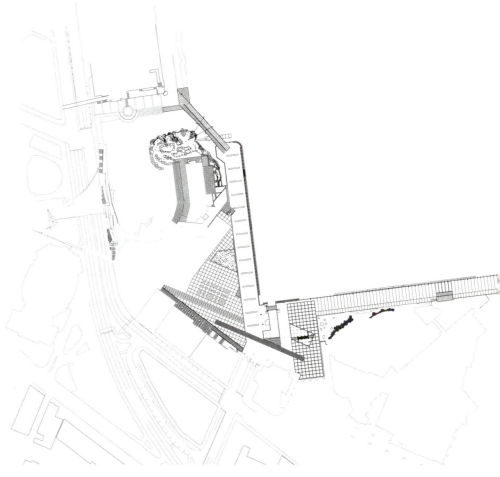

Greerton Village Upgrade, Tauranga
Isthmus Group Ltd

Greerton Village is a suburban shopping centre forming the main southern gateway to Tauranga, the provincial capital of the Bay of Penty 2 hrs southeast of Auckland. The inception of the 'Village' was born from a community inspired aim to upgrade their shopping centre and cement its identity as the community heart of Greerton. Along with this was the desire to limit ribbon development and intensify the commercial area.

The Village Green forms part of a network of public green spaces throughout the site for use as both gathering and passive recreation areas in close proximity to the community facilities.

Greerton's design cues are taken from its connection with the surrounding hinterland of the Kaimai Ranges and Welcome Bay Hills. Organic forms feature strongly in the design detailing, including free form paving bands, specially crafted bollards and street lights, and natural stone walls with intricately detailed mosaic tiling, providing splashes of colour and vibrancy.

← Plan of Greerton Village Square.
↓ Schools out... the local school children spill out into the village.

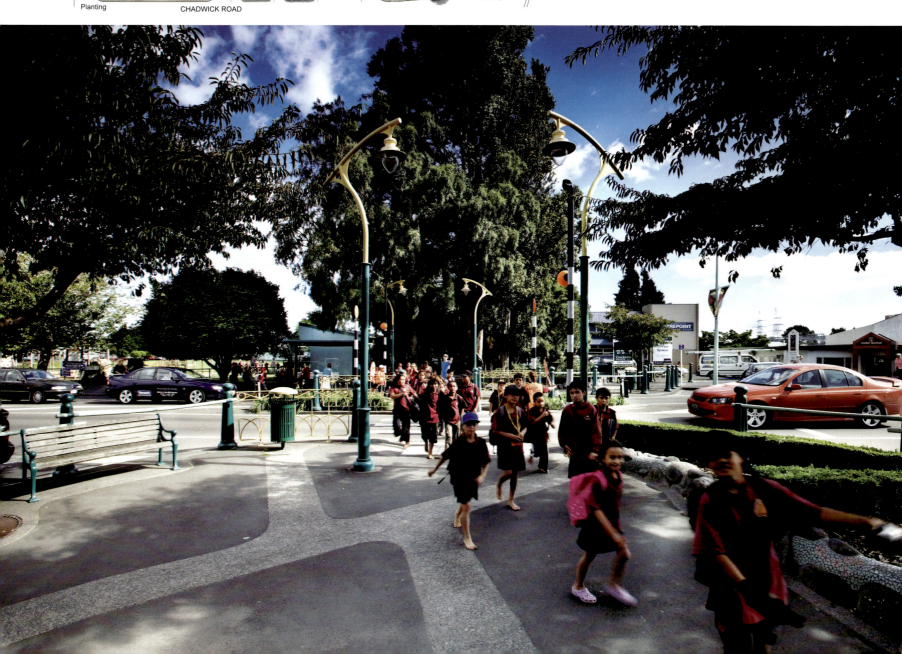

↖ & ↑   A staircase with timber landings provides a dramatic pedestrian entrance in the village and also serves as a connection between the village and upper suburbs.
↗   The central village green provides space for passive recreation and relaxation.
→   A small lawn forms part of the village green network.
↓   A walkway weaves between the village and the upper suburbs.

← "Art nouveau" inspired streetlights light up the village at dusk.
↑ The stage for outdoor festivals.
↘ Memorial plaques are set into the stonewalls.
↓ Natural stone walls with splashes of colourful mosaic tiling.

client
Tauranga District Council
other key consultants
Connell Wagner
location
Chadwick St, Tauranga, New Zealand
completion
1999
photography
Simon Devitt

Malvern City Square, Melbourne
Rush \ Wright Associates

Malvern City Square is positioned in a distinct location at the junction of two main roads in one of the highest points in the City of Stonnington. The need for a re-design of the site arose from the issue of water leakage in the underground carpark below the City Square.

The new design by Rush\Wright Associates addressed the existing problems on site and created a City Square which is immediately recognisable forming a local civic focus. The refurbishment has recently been completed receiving wide praise from the council, shop owners and the public.

The new design has increased the civic presence of the square expanding and opening up the upper level, providing large areas for gathering and functions as well as intimate areas for relaxation. The re-location of the heritage listed 'Sun God' and 'Moon God' statues by Paul Juraszek, together with new tram shelters on High Street emphasise the nature of the square and its link to surrounding streets. A more defined link to the Town Hall is achieved by two rows of pleached trees and universal access to the upper level.

The design has come to life through the use of granite pavers in three tones, new steel mesh planters, defined areas of grass and vegetation, key lighting and the activation of the upper level.

→ View over the new stainless steel mesh planters towards Malvern Town Hall.

↖ The square remains accessible at all hours through the use of new lighting and by expanding the café area on the upper level.

↑ The existing 'Sun God' and 'Moon God' sculptures were an integral part of the design and help to define the main entrance on High Street.

→ New stainless steel mesh planter and handrail. Parthenocissus species will eventually cover the planters and create seasonal colour changes.

↓ Town Planning submission.

← Dusk in the square highlighting the use of new pole lights and uplighting to the existing Plane trees along High Street.

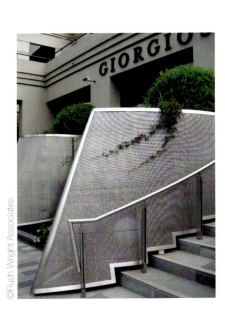

client
City of Stonnington
other key consultants
Steenson Varming,
JMP Engineers;
JA DODD (Contractor)
location
Malvern, Melbourne, Victoria, Australia
completion
2006
photography
David Simmonds, unless stated

Maddern Square, Melbourne
Rush \ Wright Associates

Maddern Square is the first built outcome of a long-planned series of public space upgrades proposed for Central Footscray. The Square uses a playful approach in creating a new public focus for this important central activity district for inner Melbourne, providing useable green space and plaza areas suited to flexible use.

The project draws on formal techniques such as level changes, walls and bollards to demarcate zones for vehicular and pedestrian traffic. Upper and lower levels also serve to divide the space programmatically. A concrete ramp provides access, connection and a space for play between these areas.

The open paved plaza to the south west end of the square provides an area for occasional events, performances, street stalls and outdoor seating/dining area.

An active interface with Chambers Street is created with the plaza extending across the street and laneway creating a permeable edge between the shared vehicle and pedestrian zone. Disc shaped bollards define the vehicle access and provide play platforms at the western edge of the square.

The design includes numerous seating opportunities in both sunshine and shade. All of these were custom-designed for the project by the rush\wright associates design team. In some instances these also form boundaries between vehicle traffic in the laneway and pedestrian areas. Through the implementation of this robust, witty and inviting design, a once neglected park at the back of a suburban centre has been unpretentiously transformed into a valuable community space.

awards
National Urban Design plans & ideas Award for planning excellence;
Planning ministers Award for Melbourne 2030 implementation;
2007 CCAA National Public Domains Awards, Precincts Category Winner.

↓ The timber topped seating wall along the plaza edge provides a stage platform for performances, play and seating overlooking activities in the Square.

← The layout of the space is simple with a number of key elements that are enriched by the use of subtle details and minimal use of bold colour.

✓ The redevelopment of the square provides a catalyst for improvement of the surrounding urban fabric and diversification of use and improved interaction with the backs of the retail premises fronting on to the square..

✓✓ Existing trees frame the northern edge of the square and provide shade to the new lawn.

← Sculptural disk forms function as traffic barriers and offer opportunities for seating and play.
↑ Articulated concrete seating walls define the edges to the shared pedestrian/vehicle link along Chambers St.
↓ Madden Square Concept Design.

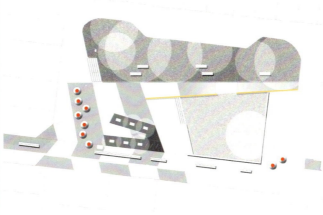

client
Maribyrnong City Council
other key consultants
Steensen Varming
location
Footscray, Melbourne, Victoria, Australia
completion
2006
photography
Michael Wright

CentrePort Stage A, Wellington
**Wraight + Associates Ltd
with Studio of Pacific Architecture**

Stage A of CentrePort's redevelopment commences the process of integrating a portion of the working harbour back into Wellington's urban fabric, the genesis of a new urban fringe at the Harbour's edge: Harbour Quays. Providing a permeable network of streets and open spaces, the scheme integrates the existing infrastructure of the port grid into the adjacent city grid, improving connection with the city and providing a pedestrian friendly network for future Harbour Quays development. CentrePort Stage A forms the northern end of the continuous city foreshore extending from Oriental Bay, through Waitangi Park and around Taranaki Wharf to the port. The proposed CentrePort redevelopment is approximately 6.5 hectares, with diverse programmatic uses from business, retail and port facilities to recreational parks with an emphasis on pedestrian permeability. Water sensitive urban design principles are integral to storm water infrastructure. Bio retention swales, rain-gardens, bio-retention tree-pits and reticulated storage areas for use in irrigation are implemented site-wide. These elements contrast the project's robust material palette that reflects the port's large-scale, industrial aesthetic.

↑ Pocket park at night.

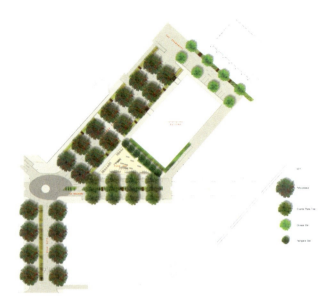

↑ Plan of Centreport Stage A.
→ Swale section.
↘ Kerb and planting detail.
↓ View from within site showing swales and lighting.

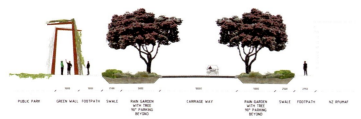

HINEMOA STREET

↑↑ Street section.
↑ Pocket park.
↗ Wind shelters / plant-climbing frames.
↘ Seat and screen detail.
↓ Swale and 'bridge' detail.

client
Centreport Wellington
other key consultants
Architects: Studio of Pacific Architecture,
Engineers: BECA.
location
Centreport, Wellington, Aotearoa New Zealand
completion
2006
photography
Wraight + Assocoates Ltd.

James Place Upgrade, Adelaide
HASSELL

James Place is one of Adelaide's quaint little open laneways connecting pedestrians between Grenfell Street and Rundle Mall. It has a character reminiscent of a European laneway, with its individual shopfronts, narrow width, and varied buildings. As part of the Rundle Mall Master Plan adopted by Adelaide City Council, it is identified as a major pedestrian street.

Adelaide City Council engaged HASSELL in a very short timeframe to review a proposed design for the paving upgrade of the street. HASSELL collaboratively engaged with Council staff, engineers, and James Place traders in an urban design process to determine the design approach of the paving materials. By interpreting the paving hierarchy being developed by Adelaide City Council, the paving design consists of economical semi polished concrete pavers, with local Adelaide stone, Kanmantoo, as a highlight. The upgrade has been well received by the traders and shoppers alike. The Council has been impressed with the strategy of mixing materials dependent on street hierarchy, whilst allowing the design standard to be improved immensely. HASSELL demonstrated that good urban design practice is not always about expensive materials, but achieving a good design outcome through a well-informed process, based on material selection, site context and consultation.

Function and Performance

UrbanStone concrete pavers, coupled with feature inlays of Kanmantoo stone, were selected as the simple paving palette. A modular approach to the design allowed maximum flexibility in a narrow laneway featuring staggered building facades with a central drainage swale.

UrbanStone was selected as the main material based on a number of functional and performance based requirements including:
— quality of pavers;
— finishes- a selection of milled, semi milled and honed surface finishes achieving different effects at different times of the day;

awards
2007 CCAA Public Domain Awards.

↑ James Place on a weekday at lunchtime.

— a small section of the pavement was required to be trafficable.

Aesthetics

Several options were developed to investigate the design opportunities associated with the laneway's hierarchy within the Rundle Mall Master Plan area. A simple paving design with several material options was explored. This included insitu concrete, concrete unit pavers, asphaltic concrete, and stone.

The end result is a canvas of base material of milled UrbanStone (medium grey) with a central drainage swale comprising honed, large aggregate UrbanStone (dark grey – black) with highlight banding at approximately 5 m of a local feature stone, known as Kanmantoo stone. This stone was selected as it is a feature of the recently rejuvenated North Terrace project and signals a link between the Rundle Mall retail core and the North Terrace cultural precinct.

The banding assists in creating a constant rhythm.

Economy

An economical approach to the procurement of the upgrade was paramount for Adelaide City Council. With a limited timeframe, an easily procurable product was required. UrbanStone was selected due to the combination of a quality finish, availability, function, performance and long term availability for replacements.

Durability

UrbanStone has proven to be a durable, high quality yet functional surface finish.

Construction Techniques

The timeframe for construction was short – before the Christmas retail period in 2005. James Place retailers were concerned about loss of trade, so a construction programme was prepared to ensure access to all businesses with a minimum of disruption. Construction was finished on time. The modular design and the obviating of cutting pavers assisted in the quick construction timeframe.

Traffic Management or Calming

A small section was required to be trafficable due to a car park entrance on James Place from the Grenfell Street end and also emergency/service vehicle access. The pavement design is therefore different in this zone, however, the surface design is not.

Overall Significance to the Public Domain

We achieved an outstanding built outcome through simple, clear graphics and design proposals to change the type, colour and size of pavers to improve the aesthetic and performance of the pavement. Together with Council's Urban Design Unit and Council's engineers, we have been able to use the urban design process to raise the design standard of pavement replacement programmes and have begun a process of design reviews within Council. Elected Members, James Place traders and Council staff have all expressed their enthusiasm for the new pavement design and are impressed with the result. We are now reviewing other opportunities with Council in the Rundle Mall area.

The design is now a template for all of Adelaide's laneways and will assist in creating a common design approach to the public domain.

Innovative Use of Concrete

Concrete pavers were selected for numerous reasons as outlined above. The resultant design is now being rolled out across Adelaide's laneways as Council is very pleased with the adaptability of the design and performance of the UrbanStone pavers.

← James Place in the evening.
↑ Simple, bold detailing and hierarchy of materials.
↗ Durability of the chosen material was a critical performance factor.
↘ A varied built form required a bold and simple design.
↓ Night view.

client
Adelaide City Council
other key consultants
Principal Civil and Hydraulic Consultant: Parsons Brinckerhoff;
Principal Contractor: Catcon;
Community Consultation: Janet Gould
location
Adelaide, Australia
completion
2006
photography
Ben Wrigley

Institutional and Commercial

The British Embassy, Sana'a, Yemen
Coe Design Landscape Architecture

A new Embassy which is located in the diplomatic district of Sana'a. The pavilion-style building is set on a sloping site within extensive grounds. The altitude of the site and its location near the base of mountains creates a microclimate; intensely dry but with periodic heavy rainfall in the short rainy season. At night there are low temperatures and the site is exposed to northerly winds.

The landscape strategy was defined by the need to create shelter within the site, to lessen the open aspect, to reduce exposure from prevailing winds and to mitigate soil loss. The grounds will be sheltered from the wind and open aspect with a screen of forestry trees and under storey. The shelter belts of selected indigenous forest plants require low levels of water once established. The planting is zone-based, those requiring more watering close to the building, drought tolerant species around the perimeter.

The masterplan takes full advantage of the slope across the site to create separate ground-floor access to each floor. The public spaces within the embassy grounds have open views. The private areas are set within walled terraces and individual enclosed gardens.

At the outset the concept for the Embassy grounds was to be a showcase the excellence of British design and an interpretation of the traditional design principals of Moorish / Islamic Gardens that are centuries old and often considered as an origin for the design of gardens. The site was planned in accordance with the theme of the Paradise Garden giving four distinct character zones of varying levels, privacy and shelter. The garden designs innovatively interpret the traditional Yemeni garden as a series of terraced gardens enclosed by mud walls.

Extensive research was undertaken in conjunction with the General Department of Forestry and Desertification Control for the choice of indigenous forest trees and with the Yemeni Ministry of Agriculture and Irrigation for the appropriate types of

awards
2007 International Award, RIBA;
2007 Greenleaf Sustainability Award.

→ The capital of the Yemen, Sana'a is set in the mountains at 2200 metres.
↘ Sketches showing the vehicle drop off area.
↘↘ Native plants taken from local cuttings and seeds being grown-on on site.
↓ The model shows the potential for shade and protection from the wind when the trees and planting are mature.

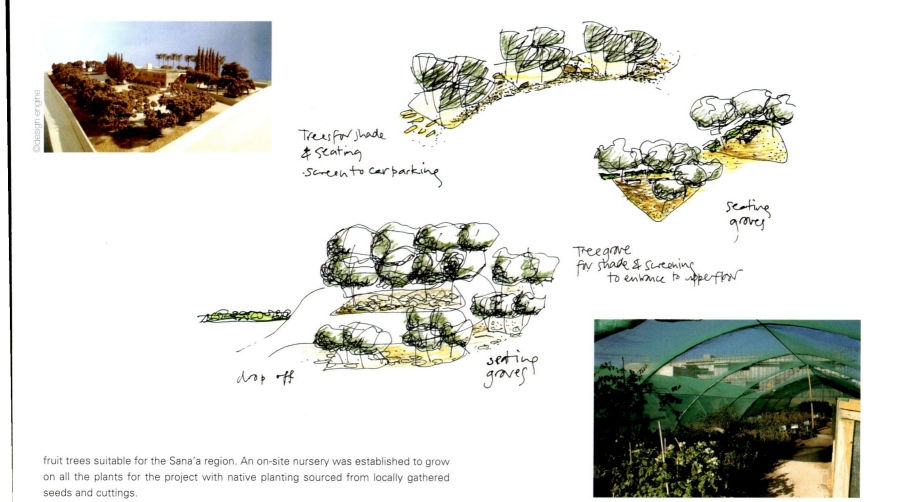

fruit trees suitable for the Sana'a region. An on-site nursery was established to grow on all the plants for the project with native planting sourced from locally gathered seeds and cuttings.

↑   The walls provide shelter from the wind.
↑↑ The garden walls were constructed using local materials and techniques unique to the Sana'a area.
↗   Drifts of grasses and flowering plants provide contrasts in colour and texture.
↘   Plants that are closer to the embassy require more watering than the plants set around the perimeter of the grounds.
↓   In the year since completing the building works the native planting has established and is thriving.

↖ The plants in the wall garden are protected from the extremes of temperature and wind.
↑ Contrasting materials: Dressed stone, concrete steps and mud walls.
↓ Colour and texture are important features in the gardens.
↙ Further away from the building the plants are more drought tolerant and require less watering.
← Many of the trees recently planted will give a greater vertical accent to the gardens over time.

client
Her Majesty's Government, The Foreign & Commonwealth Office
other key consultants
Architects: Design Engine;
Engineers: Whitby Bird.
location
The Diplomatic District, Sana'a, Yemen
completion
November 2006
photography
Coe Design Landscape Architecture unless stated

Whitireia Polytechnic, Porirua
Wraight + Associates Ltd

awards
2006, Bronze Award, New Zealand Institute of Landscape Architects.

Wraight and Associates have provided master planning for the Whitireia Polytechnic campus in collaboration with Athfield Architects Limited. The Library Learning Centre is the second project generated by the master plan to be realised. Whitireia Polytechnic Campus is located on the southern edge of Porirua Harbour. The landscape narrative has been choreographed in close relationship with the development of the Library Learning Centre. The concept of the 'housed waka' (waka: traditional Maori canoe) is reiterated in the sunken wetland, a gouged depression tracing the waka's pathway from sea to shelter. The densely planted wetland, reminiscent of the pre- reclamation harbour provides a receptacle for stormwater runoff from the new car park located to its north. The site is totally reclaimed, consisting of a 4m profile of anaerobic clays (and rubbish) over harbour silts. Salt penetrates the clay as it dries during summer, causing salinity issues throughout the site. In addition, Whitireia is exposed to strong northerly, salt laden winds. The Porirua Harbour is a highly modified and ecologically depleted environment. The master plan strategy for this site is to utilise a fairly impermeable ground to create a wetland character reflecting the site's ecological history and provide habitat for the regeneration of native flora and fauna. This stage of the Whitireia landscape works comprises a landscape framework that interprets the site's cultural and natural heritage, acknowledging and respecting its harbourside location. The network of varying spatial experiences affords the project not only amenity and sensorial stimulation but also mediates the affect of site generated stormwater run off and wind. East- west shelter belts define a directional structure while also providing shelter. Where possible the design interventions have made physical reconnections between the site and the harbour.

↓ View across wetland towards Porirua Harbour.

→ View towards Library Learning Centre over sunken wetland.
↘ Rain garden planting detail.
↓ Whitireia Library Learning Centre plan.

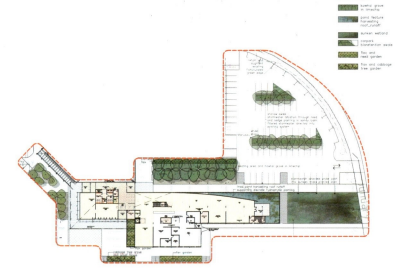

↑ Roof water catchment pond along 'housed Waka' Learning Centre.

← Sunken wetland weir detail.

client
Whitireia Polytechnic
other key consultants
Architects: Athfield Architects Ltd;
Engineers: SKM.
location
Porirua, New Zealand
completion
2006
photography
Wraight + Associates Ltd.

Deakin Central Precinct, Melbourne
Rush \ Wright Associates

The landscape for the Deakin Central Precinct forms part of a program to develop new facilities at Deakin University's Burwood Campus. It includes the design of a campus plaza enclosed by four new buildings by H2O Architects, a graphic connection to the adjacent Gardiners Creek and links to a future development site.

A large deck opens to the north of the buildings and links with grass mounds that play on scale, creating an oversized swale and reconsiders the traditional campus typology of "formal grassed square" through grading. Mounded planting and tree ferns connect the campus with a planned extension underneath a new bridge.

Planted swales run between the mounds and they collect, store and treat stormwater before it is discharged into the creek. The sensitive handling and treatment of stormwater is one of the key Environmentally Sensitive Design initiatives pursued for this project. Other initiatives include minimal use of irrigation, specification of indigenous plants and better provisioning for public transport.

The Deakin Central Precinct is defined by a careful use of materials both to reference the adjacent building facades and as a means to redefine the campus typology for a contemporary university.

↓ The concrete terrace terminating the southern edge of the eastern grass mound adds a formal dimension to the landscape concept.

← The timber terrace references the material selection of the surrounding building facades and creates a visual link between the landscape and the architecture.

↙ Looking south west towards the multi award winning architecture by H2O Architects.

↙↙ Planted swales along the grass mounds collect and treat stormwater.

↓ Looking towards the façade of the main teaching building with eastern grass mound and concrete terrace in the foreground.

→ Deakin Central Concept.

client
Deakin University
other key consultants
Architects: H2O Architects;
Civil & Hydraulic Engineers: Rimmington & Associates;
AHW Consulting Engineers (Vic) Pty Ltd;
Engineers: Meinhardt (Vic) Pty Ltd.
location
Burwood, Melbourne, Victoria, Australia
completion
2006
photography
Michael Wright

Circle on Cavill, Gold Coast
Place Design Group

Circle on Cavill is compromised of two residential towers integrated with a substantial commercial and retail precinct and located within the heart of the Gold Coast's, Surfers Paradise. Circle provides its residents with an integrated environment than can satisfy their everyday lifestyle needs.

As a renewal project within the historical heart of Surfers Paradise, Circle has successfully integrated a communities overriding need for urban consolidation and quality urban spaces servicing both the public and private realm.

The visually stunning and iconic high rise residential development is an award winning example of layered mixed use retail spaces at a street level, commercial and home offices over the next two levels and finally residential apartments and communal recreational facilities over a total of 66 floors.

With three streetscape frontages Circle is well connected and easily accessible. Entries are clearly identified and maintain vistas and sight lines that promote visual interest and interaction with Circle's quality and well defined spaces. At a ground level a true sense of place is achieved through architectural curvature, nodal plazas, and visual connectivity throughout the integrated civic spaces.

With glamour, spirit and diversity pf Circle on Cavill is a new generation mixed use precinct that is revolutionising the coasts metropolitan pastimes.

awards
2007 UDIA Qld – Urban Renewal;
2007 Gold Coast City Council Urban Design Awards
  (Built Work & Sue Robbins Awards).

↑ Urban tropical planting on ground level plaza.

← Main ground level plaza axis.
→ Private tower open area.
↘ Feature light column in central plaza.
↓ Ground level plaza with feature light column.

← Entry to main plaza with waterfeature and public artwork.
↑ Water wall with cascade.
→ Circle on Cavill towers.
↘ Feature entry sculpture.
↓ Water wall with cascade detail.

client
Sunland Group
other key consultants
Architect: Peddle Thorp
Engineer: Hyder Consulting
Construction: Sunland Construction
location
Surfers Paradise, Queensland, Australia
completion
2006
photography
Denise Yates; Sunland

Gate City Osaki, Tokyo
Thomas Balsley Associates

Gate City Osaki is a mixed-use development that includes residential, office and retail space. Its main entry plaza and public garden/cafe serves shoppers, workers, and visitors, as well as the adjoining residential neighborhood.

The Entry Plaza creates the project's "public face" and is scaled with the buildings, the pedestrian activity of the adjacent neighborhood and the nearby railway. A stand of poplar trees, bisected with a diagonal path and geometric water channels, forms a dramatic counterpoint to a sculpture of tapered orange columns tilted in random directions, trapping the visitor in a provocative dialogue between the natural and man-made. At night, the grove of trees and stone monoliths are illuminated, and the water channels and pool glow with refracted light, providing a memorable foreground silhouette to the illuminated frosted glass entry building of Gate City. An orange metal grill buffers the landscape from the motor court.

The North Garden links the various Gate City buildings to each other, as well as to the adjacent residential neighborhood, situated across a canal. Its terraces, punctuated with lines of water, lawn panels, and light, provide relief from the surrounding architecture, with each offering different outdoor experiences and levels of intimacy. Three organically shaped sculpture follies provide sheltered vantage points of the canal and back to the garden. Each folly is inspired by a plant species and provides varying degrees of spatial enclosure. Closer to the atrium, large paved areas accommodate event seating and the cafe tables served by a glowing glass kiosk.

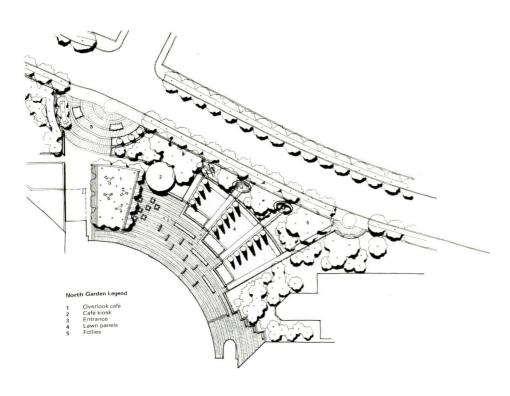

North Garden Legend

1. Overlook café
2. Café kiosk
3. Entrance
4. Lawn panels
5. Follies

↑ North Garden plan.
↗ Aerial view of the North Garden.
↘↘ Illuminated Carex folly blades.
↘ The chartreuse yellow Carex folly provides a dramatic contrast in the midst of muted trees and shrubs.
↓ Carex folly blades piercing the sky.

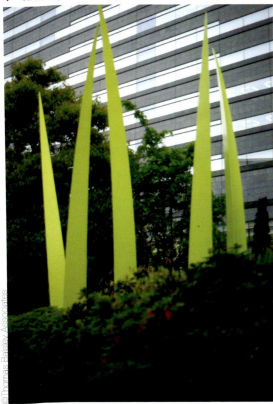

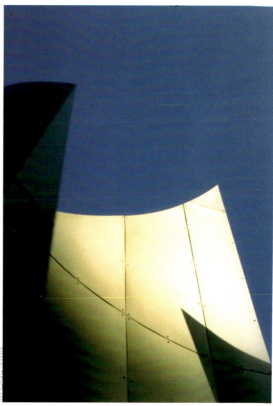

← Glass-block runnel leading to Calla folly and perforated seating.
↑ Calla folly reaching out to the sky.
↓ Calla folly view from the Japanese Garden.

↑ View out to the follies in the North garden.
↗ Dining area in the North Garden.
↓ Phragmites folly's spacing and slant suggest the force of blowing wind.

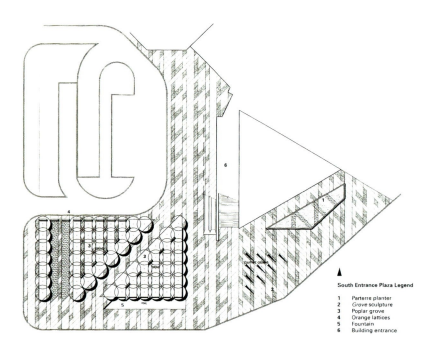

South Entrance Plaza Legend

1. Parterre planter
2. *Grove* sculpture
3. Poplar grove
4. Orange lattices
5. Fountain
6. Building entrance

↑ South garden plan.
↗ Aerial view of the South garden.
↓ Through the dense poplar trees, a visitor can catch a glimpse of the orange Grove sculpture..

↖ Aerial view of the groves with the orange panels along the drop-off area.
↑ Tree grove at the south entrance.
↗ Orange lattice panels provide a foil for the auto drop-off area.
↘ South entrance view at dusk.
← Pedestrians entering the south entrance are flanked by the Grove sculpture on the right.

client
Mitsui Fudosan Co., Ltd.
other key consultants
Architect: Nikken Sekkei;
Lighting Engineering: LPA Inc.
location
Tokyo, Japan
photography
Thomas Balsley Associates & Kokyu Miwa

Spy Valley, Marlborough
Wraight + Associates Ltd

awards
2005 Silver Award, New Zealand Institute of Landscape Architects.

The landscape works surrounding Spy Valley Wines were undertaken in recognition of both its wider and more immediate contextual landscapes. The wider landscape of the Waihopai "Spy" Valley is vast and elemental; a wide plain defined by two distinctive ridge systems, one blue and one brown. The site's immediate context is one of horticultural ordering against the industrial nature of the vineyard architecture. The building complex incorporates wine making facilities, tasting rooms, offices and a function area. On approach, the horizontal and repetitive nature of the building is mirrored in the fence design. This open, panelled fence leads to a solid precast wall, with signage incorporated, framing the entrance. A skewed grid of Oak trees structuring the car parking area leads into an entrance promenade articulated by a linear water feature. Stormwater from the car park is collected and filtered through large tree pits, re-charging ground water supplies. The water feature is fed via a series of open channel downpipes which collect rainwater from the roof. Overflow is managed by the transference of excess water beneath the promenade into a perpendicular arrangement of shallow swales leading out into the surrounding vineyard. Linear plantings of Juncus along the length of the swales connect to the wider horticultural context of the vineyard and ensure both functional and aesthetic use of stormwater is continued. Locally sourced river stone in combination with simple steel, timber and concrete elements comprise a simple materials palette that is responsive to the tonal variances of the surrounding valley. Planting baskets in the pond are designed and laid out to reflect the pixelated graphic of the Spy Valley Wines label. The vineyard tasting room opens on to an informal seating area beneath a free standing pergola, providing prospect out over the vines to the distant hills.

↑   Entrance.
↗   Horticultural ordering.
↓   Entrance promenade.

↑ Skewed grid and site stone form carpark spaces.
↗ Linear planting of juncus.
↓ Stormwater collected in carpark.

↑ Swales connect to the wider horticultural context.
↗ Shade structure.
↓ Perforated planters.

client
Spy Valley Wineries
other key consultants
Architects: Tennent Bevin Slessor
location
Marlborough, New Zealand
completion
2003
photography
Wraight + Assocoates Ltd., Bevan Slessor (Arch)

– 85 –

Osaka World Trade Center
Thomas Balsley Associates

Designing the parks and plazas for the new Osaka World Trade Center's public areas presented a number of challenges. Thomas Balsley Associates joined the design team at a point when many of the decisions about the physical structure of the development had already been made. Seizing opportunity from spatial and structural constraints, the firm welcomed the chance to explore the space's potential, to create a park-like atmosphere in which diverse urban users would feel comfortable, and to welcome the base of what is now one of Osaka's tallest buildings.

The greatest challenge to creating a park at the foot of the World Trade Center was rows of concrete ventilation towers thrusting up from an underground parking garage. Mr. Balsley imaginatively reshaped and incorporated these unsightly intruders into elaborate and intriguing fountain features. Those in the North Garden have been transformed into a performance stage structure while the six in the South Plaza appear as stainless steel cones with perforations for ventilation rising out of an elevated lagoon setting. Set in a mist pool and glowing red at night, these cones provide an astonishingly beautiful and surreal sight for World Trade Center visitors while continuing to serve their ventilation function.

As in most of Mr. Balsley's work, water plays a primary and highly visible role in the design of the Osaka World Trade Center's parks and plazas. Its recurrent use reflects his strong belief in water's regenerative, cleansing and cooling force, as well as its muffling of invasive traffic noises that shatter the calm that is sought in urban parks. In spite of the structural constraints of occupied space below the park and extensive ventilation requirements, Mr. Balsley's design created a green park environment that surrounds and is accessible from the World Trade Center tower's All Weather Park and retail facilities. By slightly elevating the park, Mr. Balsley was able to provide extensive planted areas without containers, as well as numerous intriguing displays of falling water.

awards
16th Osaka Machinami Award

The World Trade Center Building, also known as Cosmos Tower, is the centerpiece of Cosmo City, a new mixed-use development along Osaka's harbor front. The tower's base is dedicated to public spaces including a major retail center which, along with the adjoining Asian Trading Center, attracts visitors and shoppers from the area as well as thousands of office workers. The public open spaces consist of a huge indoor-outdoor atrium space (Fespa) and two connecting outdoor spaces (South Plaza and North Garden).

The distinctive stainless steel cone sculptures resting in South Plaza's fountain help to define the street level image and stylistic tone for the entire project. Their random perforations allow light and steam emissions that make an unforgettable impression on visitors and passersby. Aside from their striking sculptural qualities, the cones function as ventilators for the center's mechanical space below. Sunlight washes the plaza's circular café terrace and crescent-shaped cascade. Framed with a simple planting palette, the curvilinear upper pool is accentuated with mist jets and has been raised one meter to guarantee visual and audio buffering of the street's activities.

Leading directly out from Fespa's main floor, the North Garden features a paved performance area and additional intimate garden areas. They also have been elevated one meter both to maximize planting soil depth above the structural slab below and to provide stadium seating for programmed events. Two illuminated glass block towers provide a visual focal point and will serve as stage settings for larger performances to come.

↑ The café terrace is edged by the raised fountain and buffered from the street.
↓ Bird's eye view of the south plaza.

↑ A pine bough against the mist fountain reflects the Asian influence.
↗ The illuminated ventilation cones strike a dramatic pose as the project's icons.
↘ Water from the raised basin slides down a polished granite slope interrupted by stainless pipes.
↘↘ Distinctive red spheres edge the lower basin.
↓ The rows of six ventilation cones create a sculptural edge along the street.

↑ The tight stepping slope prvides soft casual waves along the crescent edge.
↘ Illuminated glass cubes support the stage overhead structure and provide fresh air ventilation to the mechanical rooms below.
↓ Geometric landscape forms and paving establish the north garden design language.

client
World Trade Center Associates
other key consultants
Architect: Nikken Sekkei
location
Osaka, Japan
photography
Thomas Balsley Associates

Jimbocho City, Tokyo
Thomas Balsley Associates

Situated in central Tokyo in the university and publishing district, this mixed-use development project sets new urban streetscape guidelines for its immediate neighborhood. Thomas Balsley Associates was asked to design a series of public plazas, the entire streetscape surrounding the project, and a roof garden for the residential tower.

The designers developed a language of sweeping curved walls that vary in height across the entry plaza. These walls direct pedestrians and views across the plaza and toward the building entry while also staging a provocative dialogue between the grid and the organic. A large crescent shaped 'berm' sculpture continues the geometry of these curved walls and encloses the entry plaza with a narrow silhouette of water and color.

Large panels of groundcovers and shrubs continue the geometry of the buildings on the ground plane and intersect the curved walls forming enclosed gardens. Along the streetscape edges the designers developed a curved seat wall/planter element that provides a zone of sidewalk seating

← Aerial view of the plaza along the boulevard.

↑ A secondary crescent path provides a secluded area with close proximity to the fountain.

↓ Broken stone paving with powerful geometric inserts help to humanize the ground plane.

and planting, in similar modulation to that of the building geometry. A distinctive broken stone paving pattern provides a unifying carpet of texture that reconciles the building's geometry and the strong landscape elements.

The roof garden adjacent to the residential tower uses a field of elliptical forms to articulate the garden spaces. At places, these ellipses are mounded gardens contained by curved seatwalls, these shapes form 'cut-out' intimate garden spaces. The negative cut-out space provide intimate seating coves while the oval planters imposed on the mounds provide settings for a specimen tree or grove. These striking organic forms rest in a strong geometric carpet of bi-colored pavement stripes. A rich palette of materials and colors was chosen to detail this roof garden and includes colored metal screens, curved seatwalls, river stones, moss and curved metal benches, all to the delight of the occupant as well as the viewers from above.

↑ Pockets of shaded seating align the plaza edge.
→ Curving Richard Serra-like walls of the corners also accommodate project identification.
↓ Curved seat ledges emerge from the plaza planting beds.

←← Sculpture close-up.

← The Balsley Sculpture in the main plaza is a post 9-11 appeal to cultural tolerance..

↓ Lights accent the dynamic landscape forms to animate the evening setting.

↙ A wall sculpture by Tom Balsley.

client
Mitsui Fudosan Co., Ltd.
location
Tokyo, Japan
photography
Thomas Balsley Associates & Kokyu Miwa

Mount Gambier Civic Buildings Heritage Precinct, South Australia
Fifth Creek Studio

Mount Gambier is a vibrant and modern regional city, with a proud history and significant cultural institutions and buildings. The heritage integrity of this Commercial Street precinct has been maintained, while a contemporary design approach to the forecourt and clever use of materials takes this precinct beyond a historic town character.

The design solution for this project was very innovative in the way the landscape architect Graeme Hopkins of Fifth Creek Studio used elements of the heritage buildings and plantings to reintroduce these into the new pedestrian precinct. For example, parts of the decorative building quoins were carved into the pink dolomite seat supports to encourage appreciation of this architectural detailing at pedestrian level.

The paved courtyard area adjacent to the gardens provides a physical link to the main street and is also sympathetic to the heritage of the gardens through the planting of additional palms to augment the existing Cotton Palms dating from the 1880s. The heritage value of the buildings was a significant factor in creating a forecourt that enhanced the strong architectural character without intruding or dominating visually.

Commercial Street is the main vehicular and pedestrian thoroughfare through the city, and at the same time has strong cultural and historical interest. The forecourt design now allows an open view of the buildings, unlike the closed tunnel effect created by the former cluttered planting beds. Ample seating is provided for pedestrians to view the buildings at their leisure and various texture changes in the pavement identify building entry points and directional movement. A clever use of lighting, both in the paving and the pink dolomite seat bases, makes the precinct safe and interesting for pedestrians to use in the evening.

A layered sense of place has been created for this important community precinct.

awards
2005, Merit Award for Design in Landscape Architecture, Australian Institute of Landscape Architects;
2005, Minister's Award for Outstanding Contribution, Edmund Wright Heritage Award;
2005, Heritage Places (non residential), Edmund Wright Heritage Award.

← Dolomite seats.
↑ Signage interpretive.
↗ Signage directional.
↗↗ Architectural detail.
↘ Palms at night.
↓ Heritage precinct.
↙ Heritage buildings.

client
City of Mount Gambier
other key consultants
Collaborator: City of Mount Gambier for landscape and urban design;
Architect (building restoration): Chapman Herbert Architects
location
Mount Gambier, South Australia, Australia
completion
2004
photography
Spring Studio, unless stated

TarraWarra Estate, Victoria
Tract Consultants Pty Ltd

This 900+acre former dairy farm was acquired by the client in the early 1980's and has been progressively developed over a twenty-year period, with uses and activities including farming, a family retreat, a winery and a Museum of Art.

Tract Consultants prepared a masterplan for the entire property which has been progressively implemented over this time. Included in the Masterplan were provisions for the winery, vineyard layout, interconnecting road ways, dams for water supply and revegetation of environmentally sensitive areas of the largely divided farmland.

The brilliance of this project is in the sensitive integration of the facility into a complex site and set of functional working relationships between site elements in a way that reinforces and builds a strong landscape structure.

Local stone from the site was used in many features situated amongst the property. A poplar-lined entry drive creates a clear entrance and the generously landscaped lakes enhance the setting.

Tract has maintained an ongoing upkeep of the property and Tarrawarra has been transformed over a twenty-year period from a treeless dairy farm into one of Australia's premium rural properties. The Tarrawarra Estate has become known locally and internationally for its premium wines and has become a popular tourist destination.

awards
1996, Australian Institute of Landscape Architecture (AILA) Award.

← Detail of entry drive to winery and museum.
↓ Aerial photo of view of winery and museum.

↑ View from main house.
↗ View from winery.
↓ View of entry drive.

↑ Lake and winery.
↘ Entry Gates.
↓ Museum.

client
Mr & Mrs Marc Besen
key consultants for the museum
Design Architect: Allan Powell Pty Ltd (Allan Powell);
Documentation Architect: Irwin Alsop Group;
Civil: The O'Neill Group (Tino Petrucci);
Project Principle: Maudie Palmer & Associates (Maudie Palmer);
Project Manager: Canterbury Projects (David Jarm);
Quantity Surveyor: WT Partnership (William Kennedy-Cooke, Sian McKenna).
location
Yarra Valley, Victoria, Australia
completion
Ongoing
photography
Gollings

Pacific Harbour Golf & Country Club, Queensland
Place Design Group

PLACE was commissioned to provided Master Planning and Environmental services to the Pacific Harbour project and was also appointed as the Landscape Architect for the development including the Golf and Country Club and integrated residential sub-division. The 120 hectare, 600 lot project bounded on two sides by National Park has been developed in partnership with Caboolture Shire Council and the National Park Service on environmentally sustainable design principles. The golf course, clubhouse and the first two stages of the residential community have been completed.

The 18 hole championship golf course opened for play in early 2006 and in its debut year was rated the 6th best public access course in Australia by the Golf Australia magazine. The course includes a multi-function Clubhouse and Country Club facility providing a social and recreational hub for the development. This valuable asset includes social function areas and amenities for the golf course patrons along with an associated Country Club boasting sports facilities such as gymnasium, swimming pool, and tennis courts. PLACE was responsible for the landscape design of the golf course, surrounds of the Clubhouse and Country Club building and the design of its associated external facilities. PLACE also coordinated the installation of major art pieces by Urban Art Projects within the landscape.

The environmental success of work completed by PLACE is evident on site and has contributed to accolades for the golf course residential development, recently being recognised as an Environmentally Sustainable Development 'Champion Project' by the Urban Development Institute of Australia. This challenging and innovative project is a fine example of design from a multi-disciplinary approach resulting in a sustainable and responsible outcome in a sensitive and demanding location.

awards
2007 Environmentally Sustainable Development 'Champion Project', UDIA;
2007 Excellence in Sustainable Development Finalist, UDIA Qld;
2007 Australia's 6th Best Public Access Course, Golf Australia.

↑ Pandanus overlooking 18th green.
↓ Golf & Country Club entry waterfeature.

← Hole 17.
↑ Hole 17 beach bunker and lake.
↓ Hole 1 lake.
↙ Hole 1 green.

↑ Golf clubhouse.
↗ Wedding deck.

↖ Clubhouse terrace and lake.
↑ Country club entrance.
↘ Car park Water Sensitive Urban Design swales.
↓ Country club lap pool and wet wall.
↙ Country club at night.

client
QM Properties
other key consultants
Architect: Paynter Dixon
Golf Course Architect: Ross Watson
Engineer: Hyder Consulting
Construction: Paynter Dixon / Ross Watson
location
Bribie Island, Queensland, Australia
completion
2006
photography
QM Properties; Geoff Ambler; Golf Australia

Radisson Resort Fiji, Nadi
Place Design Group

PLACE Planning & Design were originally commissioned by Tabua Investments to provide Landscape Architecture services for the Denarau Beach Resort. This 5 star resort will provide a water-focused recreational experience complete with private beaches, waterslide island, day spa island and swim up pool bar.

For pure relaxation and comfort, the resort's 270 spacious guest rooms and suites combine contemporary style with a unique blend of distinctive Fijian culture. Rooms are equipped with all the expected modern conveniences, while the one and two bedroom suites also include kitchens, separate lounge and dining areas.

Surround yourself with the natural beauty of landscaped gardens, peaceful lagoons, cascading waterfalls and discover the many resort facilities on offer. Guests of all ages will be delighted in the swimming pools including a family lagoon, dedicated children's pool with UV protection shades, and private adults only relaxation lagoon area to allow you to absorb the tranquility of the tropical setting.

Escape along waterfall-lined boardwalks to Harmony Retreat built on its own private island within the resort's pool complex. An oasis, the Harmony Retreat blends contemporary design with traditional Fijian themes. Relax and indulge in the treatment rooms and be pampered by traditional therapies with a unique Fijian essence.

↓ Site Aerial.

↖ Private Beaches.
↑ Private Rock Pool Spa.
↓ Main Pool Beach.
↙ Main Pool Beach.

↖ Main Pool - Restaurant/Bar.
↑ View from Waterfall Restaurant/Bar over Lagoon.
↓ Waterslide in Kids Play Pool.
↙ Main Pool Shade Structures - Restaurant/Bar.

client
Tabua Investments
other key consultants
Architect: Ignite
Engineer: HLK Jacobs
Construction: Fletcher Constructions
location
Denarau Island, Nadi, Fiji
completion
2007
photography
Radisson

Putrajaya Shangri-La
ICN Design International

This boutique hotel with its panoramic outlook is situated at the end of the ceremonial axis that runs through Precinct 2 of the new Government Administrative City of Putrajaya.

The landscape brief was to create an ethno-botanic guest experience that will showcase the rich diversity of tropical flora found in Malaysia. The client requested that the landscape be designed to shroud the building and permeate through it.

Working closely with the architect, an 'earth sheltering' concept that allows the building to sit within a parkland frontage was developed, with landscaped balconies leading to the roof which is further concealed by groundcover planting. Some 30% of the building'ssurface is covered by planting that blends into its parkland backdrop.

The pool deck is annexed to the side of the building and the adjacent Spa Complex is also 'earth sheltered' and the roof is extensively planted.

Landscape flows into the central courtyards to extend the ethno-botanic experience right up to the door of each guest room.

The staggered building profile allows each room to have a balcony and planter. Planting climbs up the walls and trails down the building façade to create a green shroud allowing every room to have a garden view.

The lobby is designed as a 'room outside'. The filigree nature of the architecture allows guests to sit in the comfort of the lobby but feel like they are enjoying the leisure of a garden.

The garden terrace concept extends to the roof with mono-culture blocks of

awards
2007, Gold Award, Hotel Category, Institute of Landscape Architects Malaysia (ILAM).

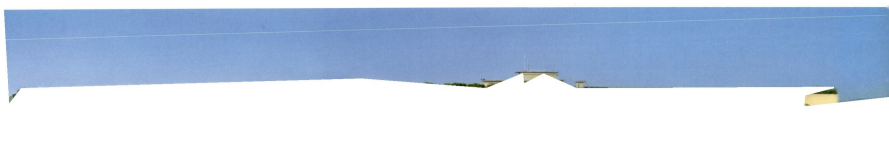

1. Visitor Carpark
2. Approach Road
3. Outdoor Terrace
4. Hotel Main Building
5. Entrance Forecourt
6. Valvet Parking
7. Spa Block
8. Pool Deck
9. Swimming Pool
10. Terrace Garden
11. Woodland Structure Planting
12. Function Lawns
13. Internal Courtyard A
14. Internal Courtyard B
15. Lobby

← Master plan.
↑ Panorama view of the hotel entrance.
↓ Lobby Fountain.
↓↓ Approach view with function lawn in foreground.

ground covers to assist in insulating the roof and controlling the thermal properties of the building.

The two courtyard atrium voids rise three and a half storeys to a linear skylight. Direct sunlight is only experienced at mid day and the courtyards are sheltered in shade for the rest of the day. The environment is reminiscent of a forest sub-canopy with the air conditioning resembling the cooler up-land forests. This inspired the courtyard design to be based on an up-land forest fern valley where the building provides the main canopy structure under which a babbling stream lined with tree ferns and ground covers runs from the end of the courtyard back to the central lobby core.

An infinity edge pool enjoys panoramic views across Putrajaya. The paving design is inspired from patterns in etchings by the Sarawakian artist Jack Ting Mui Chee. The Spa complex has a male and female facility and each room has its own private garden view.

← Spa Block.
→ Ground cover planting on the roof.
↙ Raised Garden Terrace.

← Lobby foyer in garden setting.
↑ Pool Deck with Putrajaya panorama.
→ Fin walls between balconies provide privacy and a medium up which climbers can grow.
↘ Presidential Suite Private Garden.
↓ 'Fern Valley' Courtyard.

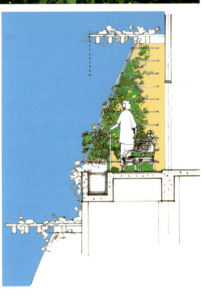

client
Perbadanan Putrajaya
other key consultants
Architect : Zaini Dubus Richez Sdn Bhd. (ZDR);
Interior Design : Rizzuan Yeoh Ong (RYO);
Civil and Structural Engineer : T&T Konsult Sdn Bhd ;
Mechanical and Electrical Engineers : Norman Disney & Young.
location
Putrajaya, Malaysia
completion
Sept. 2004
photography
Adept Studio – Kenneth Lim

Chiva Som International Spa at Khao Kho, Petchaboon
Coe Design Landscape Architecture

The first phase of the masterplanning and design for Chiva-Som International's second spa near Petchaboon in north Thailand, to complement its internationally acclaimed spa at Hua Hin on the south east coast. The 150 hectare estate for the spa and public park are located across hills in a river valley in the de-forested Khao Kho region. At 1000m above sea level the resort offers a pleasant all year round climate.

The entrance and greeting area of the resort, the 1st Phase of this large and complex project has been completed. The next phases have been started and will be completed in 2010.

The hills are being extensively replanted with trees indigenous to the area. A series of lakes are being created along the base of the valley in which the spa is spectacularly located. The steep hills surrounding the complex include rock formations and natural drainage courses. The environment of the valley is being restored to support diverse habitats, from open fresh water to forest. A system of natural trails for walking and cycling are being created around the spa.

In the process of designing the individual spaces for guest accommodation, informal outdoor dining spaces, terraces, walkways and roof terraces, we have drawn inspiration from the Lama tradition of this area of northern Thailand. Sourcing local materials wherever possible and working closely with landscape contractors to provide native trees and planting.

The emphasis has been on high quality finishes and detailing to create a unique and luxurious environment for the spa guests.

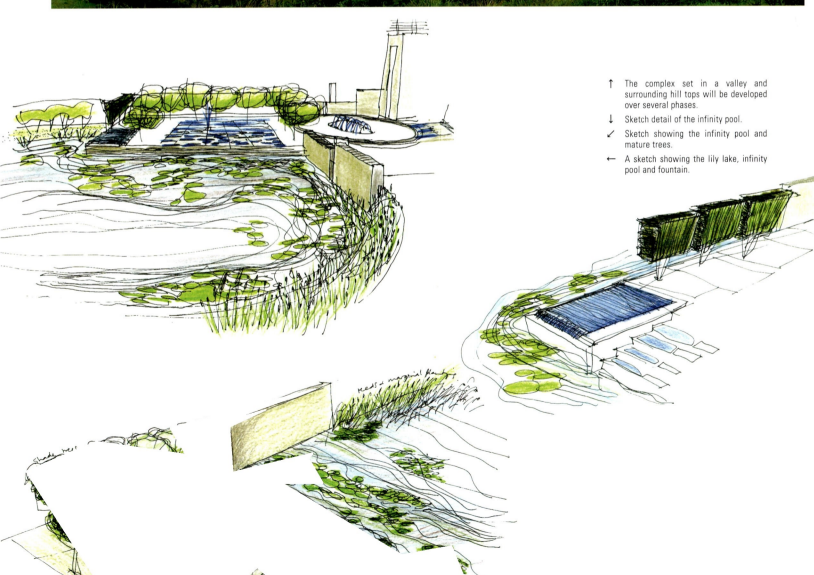

↑ The complex set in a valley and surrounding hill tops will be developed over several phases.
↓ Sketch detail of the infinity pool.
↙ Sketch showing the infinity pool and mature trees.
← A sketch showing the lily lake, infinity pool and fountain.

↑ Eye of Enlightenment.
↘↘ The waterwall.
↘ The fountain and associated rill are to the left of the infinity pool.
↓ The entrance terrace.

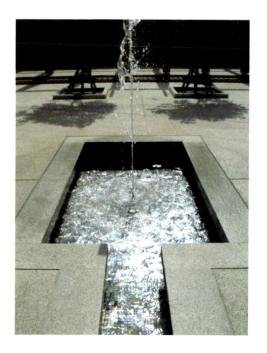

↖ The fountain at night.
↑ Known as the Eye of Enlightenment, the fountain is a central feature of the entrance complex.
↓ Pool edge.
↙ Waterfall at night.
← The rill running down the terraced paving at night.

client
Chiva-Som International
other key consultants
Architects: Syntax.
Lighting Design: Cambell Lighting Design.
location
Kho Kho, Petchaboon, N Thailand
completion
Phase 1 early 2007, other phases by 2010
photography
Coe Design Landscape Architecture unless stated

Parks and Gardens

Genesis Masterplanned Community, Queensland
Place Design Group

awards
*2007 UDIA Qld – Consultants' Excellence;
Qld and National Stormwater Industry Association
Award for Major Water Sensitive Urban Design.*

Located in the northern Gold Coast suburb of Coomera, Genesis is a revolutionary master planned residential community that through its innovative development initiatives has inevitably raised the bar for sustainable residential living.

Developer Heritage Pacific and its project consultants, PLACE Design Group has received industry recognition for their achievements in consulting excellence and sustainable development outcomes.

The estate, situated on 76ha of undulating Greenfield's, has integrated a creative blend of landscape design sustainability initiatives and an eco sensitive approach to deliver a community where residents can exist harmoniously with nature whilst also enjoying innovative communication and cost saving technologies.

While the project evolution of Genesis is one that must be credited to a large collaborative project team of consultants, PLACE has been the lead consultant for the project and has driven many of the elements and initiatives that are present on site, which make Genesis what it is today.

A visit to Genesis, will allow people to very clearly see that the quality of the estate is far above anything else within the region. This project has achieved outstanding land management and landscape outcomes in the development of the Genesis residential estate.

The vision for Genesis is based on five guiding 'pillars':

Environment / Innovation / Community / Healthy Living / Location

Through PLACE's commitment to these pillars their contribution to the project has brought a creative blend of sustainability initiatives. This eco-sensitive approach assists in the delivery of a community where residents exist harmoniously with nature whilst enjoying innovative technologies and a lifestyle revolutionizing modern living.

↑ Entry road announces the key qualities of Genesis.

← Central lakes used in the stormwater treatment process.
↓ Bird's eye view of central lake.

↖ Birds eye view of central lake and pedestrian walkway/bridge bridge.

↑ Existing trees are retained to contribute to the sustainability and habitat values.

↖ Pedestrian and cycle paths throughout provide healthy living opportunities.
↑ Streetscape incorporating Water Sensitive Urban Design.
↘↘ Entry statements.
↘ Streetscape bollards.
↓ Branded parkland bollards.
↙ Curved pedestrian walkway/bridge with angled totems.
↙↙ Pedestrian walkway/bridge.

client
Heritage Pacific
other key consultants
Master Planning & Town Planning: PLACE Design Group;
Engineer: Belleng VDM / Burchill VDM;
Environmental: PLACE Design Group;
Construction: Gary Dean Construction / Hutchinson Builders
location
Coomera, Queensland, Australia
completion
On-going
photography
Heritage Pacific

Royal Park Wetlands, Melbourne
Rush \ Wright Associates

The development of a wetland system for stormwater recycling was a key component of the Royal Park Masterplan adopted by City of Melbourne in 1998. Working with principal consultant Ecological Engineering, Rush/Wright Associates developed the design and landscape masterplan for the wetlands and surrounding open space at the western edge of the park.

Adjacent to the 2006 Commonwealth Games Athletes Village and subsequent permanent residential development. The wetlands provide recreational space in addition to water treatment capabilities.

The wetlands system consists of two linked ponds that provide natural water quality treatment and the storage of treated stormwater captured from the main drain in Park Street. Recycled water is then used for irrigation in Royal Park with clean excess water discharged to Moonee Ponds Creek and Port Phillip Bay.

→ The serpentine treatment wetland provides a natural filtration system and ornamental water body within the former hockey field..

←← Treated water is stored in this deep lagoon for reuse as summer irrigation to the surrounding parkland.
← Varying water depths and dense native planting clean stormwater through natural biological processes.
↓ Dramatic views have been created between the parkland and the adjacent freeway structures.
↙ Excess clean water overflows to the Moonee Ponds Creek on the opposite side of the freeway.

↖ Existing trees provide a shaded outlook across the wetland. The space is now a focus for both education and recreation.

↑ The wetland provides an important addition to the park's existing wildlife habitat.

→ Rocky peninsulas shape the wetlands, defining water flow and varied habitats.

← A bird hide viewing area overlooks the inlet pond.

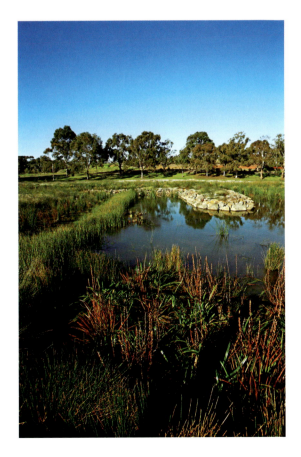

client
City of Melbourne
other key consultants
Ecological Engineering
location
Royal Park, Melbourne, Victoria, Australia
completion
2005
photography
David Simmonds, unless stated

Kota Kemuning Wetland Park, Shah Alam
ICN Design International

awards
2003, Runner-up: Professional Design Awards, Site Analysis & Planning category, Singapore Institute of Landscape Architects;
2007, Gold Award, Land Reclamation Category, Institute of Landscape Architects Malaysia (ILAM).

The Kota Kemuning Wetland is approximately 3 km long and occupies some 27 acres of land along the New Town frontage of Kota Kemuning. The original site condition was derelict land with low lying water-logged oil palm trees.

The land was unkempt, overgrown and visually unattractive as a development frontage. The challenge was to design a workable solution to up-grade the appearance of the degraded land.

The solution was not only dependant on design, but also on policy, as the land was owned by several statutory bodies who all had different requirements and objectives for their land.

The two dominant reserves, both of which ran the length of the site, were the Drainage and Power reserves. The design approach applied value engineering to a proposed concrete drain, transforming it into a free-form natural retention based wetland system. The system would involve a series of inter-linked open channel ponds, with adjacent flood and retention plains that would traverse both the power and drainage reserves. Adding variety to the more conventional conveyance based drainage approach, the more passive retention based system allowed public access to be safely incorporated within the park flood plain.

Re-designing the concrete drain provides several important benefits. Firstly, the open channel system with its capacity to flood within controlled parameters provides a huge retention capacity way above a concrete 'U' drain. The cost of the 'U' drain was estimated at around RM (Ringgit Malaysia) 10 million, while the entire wetland design, including earthworks, hard and soft landscape was built for significantly less. In addition to cost savings, the design approach is also far more environmentally sensitive providing a long term sustainable drainage system.

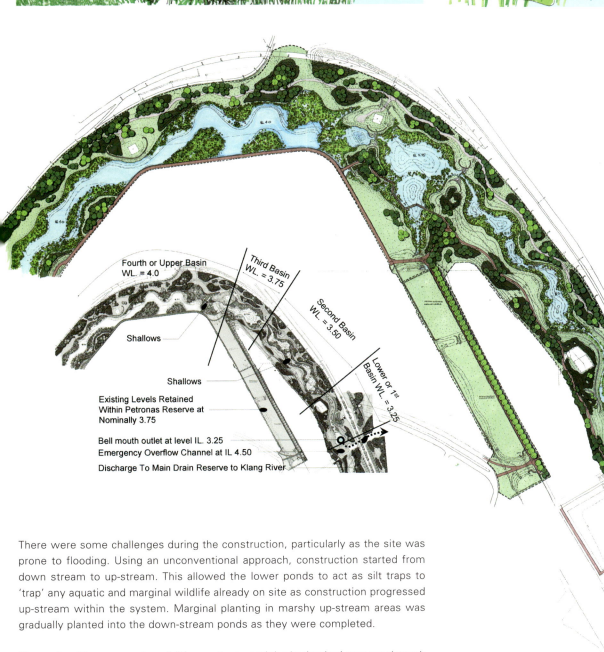

↖ Sketch visualization for the design intent of the Northern Channel.

↑ Visualisation of the Western Promenade adjacent to the Petronas Gas Reserve.

← Integrated Masterplan incorporating the wetland and upgraded approach road to the Kota Kemuning Township.

↙ The wetland is essentially 4 ponds that are an integral part of the drainage system for surface run-off that discharges from the township.

There were some challenges during the construction, particularly as the site was prone to flooding. Using an unconventional approach, construction started from down stream to up-stream. This allowed the lower ponds to act as silt traps to 'trap' any aquatic and marginal wildlife already on site as construction progressed up-stream within the system. Marginal planting in marshy up-stream areas was gradually planted into the down-stream ponds as they were completed.

The wetland is now a major wildlife sanctuary; and the 'reduction' process through the open channel system is continually improving water quality. Proposing an approach that was both economically and environmentally sustainable allows a desirable win-win scenario to take place. The clients wins because they saved money and achieved more for less; and have the added benefit of an attractive frontage to their development. The environment wins because it secures a re-instated natural eco-system. The residents win because they can enjoy a 27 acre natural park.

↑ Pond 2 in its matured state after 3 years.
↗ Pond 2 after 12 months.
↓ Pond 3 in its matured state after 3 years.

The Western Promenade after completion.

↑   Amenity marginal planting.
↗   An abundance of aquatic, reptile and wildlife has rapidly colonized the park.
↘   Western Promenade railing detail.
←, ↙, ↓   The Northern Channel after completion.

client
Hicom Gamuda Developments Sdn Bhd
other key consultants
Town Planner: AJC Planning Consultants;
Civil Engineers: Zaidun Leeng Sdn Bhd.
location
Kota Kemuning, Shah Alam, Malaysia
completion
Nov, 2002
photography
Julien Hodson-Walker

Wetland 5, Sydney Park, Sydney
ASPECT Studios Pty Ltd

ASPECT Studios were commissioned by the City of Sydney to design and document Wetland 5, the culmination of the chain of wetlands in Sydney Park. This existing area is the oldest parcel of land in Sydney Park and the only piece which remains on deep soil (rather than on fill). The project site was a wetland which was in a state of disrepair with rotting timber logs and a leaky substructure which resulted in the loss of water. The condition of the wetland was undermining the environmental benefits of the wetland system. ASPECT Studios brought extensive site knowledge to the project, having completed the detailed master plan for Sydney Park in May 2006.

The scope for the project included design development and construction of the wetland and surrounds including pathways, retaining walls, seating and shade trees. The materials selected reflect the vision of the detail master plan which was to recognise and mark this place as the culmination and holding point for the greater parks wetland system. The design of the high quality, in-situ concrete walls work as a semi circular bracket or 'frame' to the park water course. The water from wetland 5 is recirculated through out Sydney Park enabling the wetland species to flourish and attract fauna to the park. The existing mature Casuarina's and Eucalyptus on site set the character of the place (but added to the general degraded image of the area through a lack of maintenance over time). ASPECT Studios saw the opportunity to mark the upgrade of the park by inserting a simple and robust gesture which is of its time. The concrete arc sets both the infrastructure and the organisational logic of the park and provides an informal seat and edge to the wetland. Fluorescent lights (which are triggered by a light sensor which respond to the environmental conditions) are housed in the wall creating a safe and usable space whilst also being an attractor at night. Detailed hydrological and contamination issues required carefully considered design solutions from concept to construction. ASPECT Studio's scope was to build on the Sydney Park detailed master plan (completed in 2006 by ASPECT Studios + CAB Consulting) and ensure that the qualities embedded within this document were realised in

← Visualisation Plan.
↓ Insitu Concrete edge.

the built form including the wetland, retaining walls and boardwalk (the design of which relates to the existing family of decks and boardwalks seen throughout the park).

Design excellence and functional quality:
Wetland 5 has been designed to be unashamedly of its time as a contemporary park design. Its materials used, including concrete and timber are robust and appropriate for its purpose.

The design does not rely on traditional wetland motives and materials to reveal its function such as the often seen sandstone boulders and decorative artworks. The bold off form concrete arc, which defines the extent of the wetland, relates to the greater industrial context of the St Peters area and the 'industrial sublime' of Sydney Park.

The contrast of the concrete planters and wall with the fine textured wetland plants and fauna that they attract creates a rich play.

The simple gesture of the arc is the key to the design and has been maintained through the detailed master plan to construction. The arc is a clear diagram which terminates the watercourse through Sydney Park and provides bench seating along its entire length. Views to the greater landscape are framed by the screens of existing Casuarinas.

The wall is a multi-use element which houses a range of functions including:
- an edge to the wetland water body (stabilising the High Density Plastic liner for the wetland);
- a seating edge (the entire length is a generous park bench);
- lighting (fluorescent lights activated by sensors are hung under the concrete reveal to create additional safety and attractor at night);

- an edge to the circulation path (the wall is an edge to the central path and has been designed with sensitivity to existing levels and trees on site.

As this is an insertion and an upgrade to an existing park, there was a range of constraints which were sensitively dealt with. These included:
- preserving existing tree
- maintaining opportunities for existing park users by maintaining and upgrading desire lines
- resolving the hydraulic engineering issues of the wetland as well as the obvious expectation to greatly improve on the existing degraded open space.

The upgrade to Wetland 5 has provided a significantly improved wetland and park experience as well as improving safety and surveillance opportunities for passive recreation. This wetland upgrade provides Sydney Park with a clear bench mark for further upgrades in line with the detailed master plan.

The quality of the concrete work is extremely high for an in-situ off form project. The contractors M+R Constructions erected a purpose built steel gib which was moved along the arc to achieve and excellent finish. The class specified was class 2 concrete and we are pleased to see that this was achieved.

Environmental responsibility and sustainability

A wetland project by its nature alone does not simply comply with the criteria for excellence in Environmental design, though it is a good start. Wetland 5 was a wetland prior to this upgrade albeit degraded and loosing water through breaks in the substructure.

The brief to rectify the wetland gave us the opportunity to revisit the design of the Wetland 5 surrounds and extend the environmental potential.

Wetland 5 is the key to the entire wetland system (3 other wetlands throughout Sydney Park) as it is in the lowest part of the park. The water is gathered here and pumped back through the system. The wetlands have enabled significant new growth in an extremely challenging growing medium (a thin crust of soil over a rubbish tip) and as a consequence has created new eco systems which attract biodiversity (birds and other fauna) to this semi industrial park. The new native and endemic palette of plants in wetland 5 will attract a greater array of fauna and will require less ongoing maintenance.

Relevance to the profession of landscape architecture, the public and the education of future practitioners.

Wetland 5 is a contemporary example of the 'landscape cyborg'. It is a contemporary urban park underlain with significant environmental design – much of which is hidden to the eye. Wetland 5 is a relevant example of the fusion of environmental objectives and high quality design that creates a memorable and enduring parkland.

↖ Wetland edge and precast seat with wetland planting.
↑ View from boardwalk jetty towards wetland edge.
→ Lighting along wetland edge and boardwalk.

← Wetland with its native tree: Casuarina in the back, Juncus species in the front.
↑ Wetland edge and precast seat with lighting.
↗ Lighting detail is under the seat. Uses compact fluorescent lights. Light is recessed in concrete profile.
↗↗ Wetland edge showing extent of precast seat & lighting.
↘ Precast seat and lighting detail.
↓ Details of Wetland edge and precast seat.

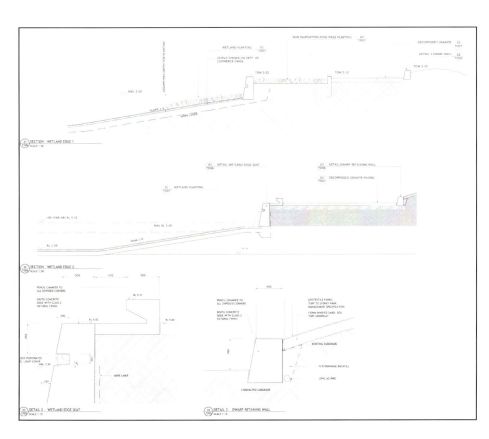

client
City of Sydney Council
other key consultants
Structural and Civil Engineers: Warwick Donnelly Pty Ltd.
location
Sydney Park, St Peters, Sydney, Australia
completion
2007
photography
Simon Wood

Ecology Park, Cibinong Science Centre, West Java
Sheils Flynn Ltd.

The Science Centre at Cibinong, West Java is the headquarters of Lembaga Ilmu Pengetahuan Indonesia (LIPI), the Indonesian Institute of Sciences. Sheils Flynn's ongoing masterplanning work promotes sustainable development, environmental education, access to nature and interpretation, creating a campus which is a model for landscape-led sustainable development in Indonesia.

The driving force behind the campus masterplan is a fundamental recognition that the success of sustainable development rests on the creation and long-term management of an interconnected network of native habitats, endemic to the site. One small valley within the campus is being developed as an Ecology Park, with new wetland habitats and a visitor centre. When complete, it will become part of an innovative botanical garden (an extension to Indonesia's world famous Kebun Raya, Bogor) which will display typical plants from the seven bioregions of Indonesia in their own habitats. The new wetland complex will be the point of entrance to the botanical garden and is designed to display plants from the Java and Bali bioregion. It is already proving to be a popular and thought provoking public landscape where people can learn about native Javanese habitats and the interrelationships between all living organisms.

Construction of a new weir across the existing small stream and careful sculpting of the valley contours created a sizable lake, with varied margins and shallows for a range of riparian planting. The valley slopes are planted as native, species-rich lowland forest, an exceptionally diverse habitat which has been dramatically reduced and degraded throughout West Java. A striking sequence of terraces and steps lead down from a new visitor's centre and car park to the lakeside where a curving boardwalk encourages visitors to cross the water to a viewing platform on the opposite bank.

Landscape restoration takes time and it is still early days for the EcoPark, but this nationally important case study describes a responsible approach to public landscape design.

← Cibinong Ecology Park - Illustrative Masterplan.
↓ The first viewpoint.
↙ The first views across the lake - this is not the ornamental 'park' landscape typical of so many Indonesian commercial developments; instead the EcoPark is designed to show visitors a variety of habitats at closehand.

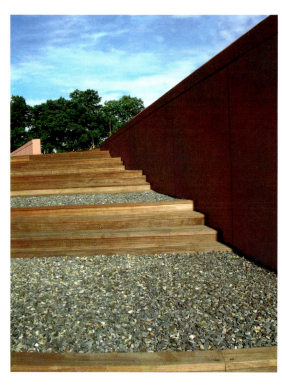

↑ Steps leading down to the water's edge.
↗ Water buffalo at the lakeside.
↗↗ View across the lake to the distant volcanoes.
↘ Lakeside viewing platform.
↓ A boardwalk curves across the lake, leading visitors through reedbeds and then out across open water to an events area.

↖ View across the lake to existing tower & vegetation. The foreground gabion wall is part of the new weir which controls levels of water throughout the Ecology Park wetlands.

↑ School children regularly visit the EcoPark.

↓ The future EcoPark – 3D Sketch.

← Waterplants and existing lakeside buildings.

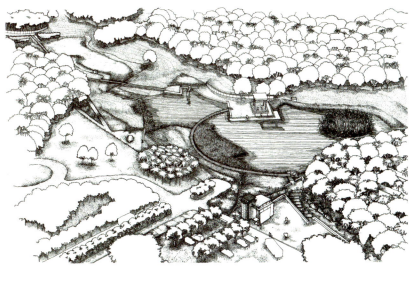

client
Lembaga Ilmu Pengetahuan Indonesia (LIPI), the Indonesian Institute of Sciences.

location
Cibinong, West Java, Indonesia

photography
Sheils Flynn

Former BP Park, Waverton, Sydney
mcgregor+partners

awards
2006 Merit Award for Design, AILA National Project Awards;
2006 landscape and ecologically sustainable development, North Sydney Council Design Excellence Award;
2005 Overall Award for Excellence, Australian Institute of Landscape Architects, NSW Chapter;
2005 Design Excellence Award, Australian Institute of Landscape Architects, NSW Chapter;
2005 National Commendation Award for excellence in precinct design of the public domain by the Cement Concrete & Aggregates Australia.

The new public parkland at the former BP site was officially opened on the 12th of March. Located on Waverton Peninsula, the site is the first of a series of waterfront areas in North Sydney to be transformed from industrial depots into public parklands. The new 2.5-hectare harbourside park is a result of the New South Wales Government's decision in 1997, to convert Waverton's three waterfront industrial sites for public use and reject their sale for residential development.

Following remediation of the site by BP Australia, mcgregor+partners landscape architects were commissioned as lead consultant to prepare detailed design drawings and oversee construction of the new park.

The Former BP Park site once housed 31 storage tanks, offices and massive concrete perimeter bung walls to prevent oil spills reaching the harbour. The design acknowledges the site's former use through the restrained composition of simple, yet robust structures. The new design celebrates the site's industrial heritage and harbour location with a series of open spaces, wetlands and spectacular viewing decks that embrace the dramatic, semi-circular sandstone cliff cuttings where the oil tanks formally stood. A combination of concrete and metal staircases wrap around the cliffs and project over the water sensitive, wildlife-attracting ecosystem found below.

As a result of the site being used for oil storage for over 60 years, it had become contaminated and in order to create the park, a variety of environmentally sustainable design initiatives were employed. Existing site soil, rather than being excavated and consigned to landfill, was mixed with imported organic matter and re-used across the site. Provenance seed stock was collected from nearby Balls Head, propagated and used as plant stock to reinstate the natural flora of the site.

↑ Northdrum end.
→ Location plan.

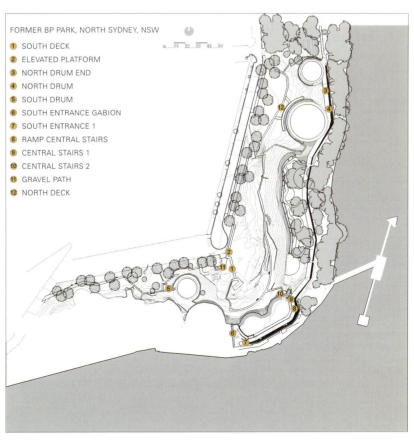

FORMER BP PARK, NORTH SYDNEY, NSW
1. SOUTH DECK
2. ELEVATED PLATFORM
3. NORTH DRUM END
4. NORTH DRUM
5. SOUTH DRUM
6. SOUTH ENTRANCE GABION
7. SOUTH ENTRANCE 1
8. RAMP CENTRAL STAIRS
9. CENTRAL STAIRS 1
10. CENTRAL STAIRS 2
11. GRAVEL PATH
12. NORTH DECK

The design incorporated an integrated stormwater collection and filtration system that directs site water into detention ponds planted with aquatic plants. These ponds filter and clean the water prior to it discharging into the harbour. The establishment of this detention system has additional benefits in that it has created new habitats for a variety of frogs as well as ducks and other bird species.

The park's defining material finishes of in-situ concrete and galvanised steel are references to the industrial past and were selected for their low-cost, low-impact and low-maintenance qualities.

Sydney harbour is at a nexus, where post-industrial lands are searching to find uses that go beyond their pure commercial potential. The Former BP Park is emblematic of the moves to reclaim the harbour foreshore for the people of Sydney while recognising the importance of retaining a site's heritage.

← Elevated Platform.
↑ Northdrum.
↗ Southdrum.

↖ Central Stairs 02.
↑ Ramp Central Stairs.
↗ Central Stairs 01.
↗↗ South Entrance Gabion.
↓ Aerial View.
← South Deck.

client
North Sydney Council
location
Larken Street, Waverton Peninsula, Waverton, North Sydney, New South Wales, Australia
other key consultants
Northrop Engineers
completion
2005
photography
Brett Boardman, Simon Wood & Brett Cornish

Twelve Apostles Visitors Centre, Victoria

Tract Consultants Pty Ltd

The Twelve Apostles, a series of colossal rock pillars ascending from the churning waters below are one of the three most internationally recognised natural features of the Australian landscape (the others include Great Barrier Reef and Uluru). Receiving 1.2 million visitors in 1999 the Twelve Apostles daily visitation varies from 1,700 to 4,500 visitors per day, and is estimated to grow at a rate of 5-9% per year.

Tract Consultants were commissioned by Parks Victoria as principal consultants for the site selection and concept planning of a tourist amenity facility at the Twelve Apostles site near Port Campbell, Victoria, Australia.

Existing conditions were notably inadequate, resulting from ad hoc upgrades of original tracks through the coastal heathland, lack of toilet facilities, poor access and insufficient parking or pedestrian circulation.

Tract's site selection and evaluation was based on a range of criteria covering visual, physical, ESD, and net environmental gain for the project. The preferred site was selected on the basis of relocating all major physical aspects of the facility to leasehold grazing land adjacent the park. The result was an increase in national park, a controlled pedestrian access, through coastal healthland, via an underpass under the Great Ocean Road to the viewing platform.

Creative application of ESD principles in respect of stormwater management, greywater retention, rainwater harvesting and recreation of natural wetlands as final water polishing played a critical role.

The study outcome was the provision of an environmentally sustainable tourist amenity facility of international significance, including interpretation and signage, toilets/rest rooms, parking for over 200 cars, twelve buses and 12 caravans / trailers, fully accessible pedestrian trails, Great Ocean Road pedestrian underpass, viewing platform and rehabilitated coastal heath parkland.

awards
2003, Australian Institute of Landscape Architecture (AILA) Award;
2004, Australian Institute of Landscape Architecture (AILA) Award.

The success of the project is the maximisation of the wild coast experience by way of a rigorous rationalisation of all programme elements, together with a sensitive and comprehensive siting and grading study, of all aspects of the facility.

↑ Aerial view of visitor centre.

← Site context on shipwreck coast.
↑ Aerial view of overall facility and the water treatment lagoon.
↗ Masterplan concept.
↓ Pedestrian underpass to viewing platform.

client
Parks Victoria
other key consultants
Architect: Greg Burgess Architects Pty Ltd;
Structural/Civil: Grogan Richards Pty Ltd;
Interpretation: David Lancashire Pty Ltd;
Ecologists: Ecology Australia Pty Ltd;
Quantity Surveyor: Slattery Australia;
Environmental Eng: C Woodward Clyde &
  Gutteridge Haskins & Davey.
location
Port Campbell National Park, Victoria, Australia
photography
Gollings

South East Asian Rainforest Immersion - The Adelaide Zoo
HASSELL

The South East Asian Rainforest Exhibit 'Immersion' is an exciting new exhibit within Adelaide Zoo and an important addition for Adelaide. Immersion 'removes the barriers', creating a landscape which transports visitors to the natural Sumatran habitats of the endangered orang-utans and Sumatran tigers. The design gives visitors an appreciation of the animals in their natural environment, providing opportunities for natural behaviour through a considered design process. Exhibiting Orang-utans, Siamangs and Sumatran Tigers, Immersion increases the enrichment for the animals and offers visitors a new insight into the rainforest ecosystems and conservation programmes in Sumatra. With the applied messages of conservation and environment, immersion conveys a strong social and environmental message through urban and landscape design.

Immersion removes the barriers between visitors and animals through creative design and innovative construction techniques. Enrichment opportunities are provided such as climbing towers, overhead climbing links ('O' lines) for the Orang-utans, water bodies and swimming areas for the Tigers and opportunities to rotate Tigers into Orang-utans' enclosure when the Orang-utans are within their night quarters. Traditional Sumatran Long House architecture has inspired the design of the central pavilion and provides a focal point for the exhibit, allowing people to congregate and to be truly immersed in the habitat of these extraordinary animals. Glass barriers and underwater viewing add to the unique character of this area, providing the Zoo and Adelaide with a world-class exhibit.

Environmental enrichment is a key feature of the design concept, ensuring that animal welfare considerations are fully addressed. Many of the design features developed by HASSELL had not previously been incorporated into an exhibit design anywhere else in the world and have set international standards for the management of orang-utans and tigers in captivity.

awards
2007 AILASA Merit Award for Design in Landscape Architecture.

Traditional Sumatran architecture has inspired the design of the hub pavilion. Recycled timber, 'Colourgrain' bluescope steel roof and a bamboo ceiling were chosen to provide an immersion experience for visitors.

← Climbing towers allow the orang utans to exhibit their natural behaviour, simulating their rainforest habitat.
→ Carta, the female orang utan brachiates the o'line.
↓ Customised 'bamboo' colourgrain fencing ensures all fixings are outside of the exhibit and will camouflage with the vegetation as it matures.

← Water is used as a primary barrier for the tigers.

↖ Central hub area allows for large crowds, evening events and general viewing.

↑ Salt wash concrete was chosen as a hard wearing surface that simulated compacted earth. Recycled timber is used for balustrades and cladding in the hub pavilion adjacent the underwater viewing at the tiger swimming hole.

↓ 'Jail safe' glazing provides visitors with an up close encounter with the endangered animals.

client
Royal Zoological Society of South Australia
other key consultants
Services Engineers: Lincolne Scott;
Principal Engineering Consultant: TMK Consulting Engineers;
Principal Contractor: Built Environs;
Cost Managers: Rider Hunt
location
Adelaide, Australia
completion
2006
photography
Ben Wrigley

Lory Loft at Jurong Birdpark, Singapore
Green & Dale Associates

Lory Loft, at Singapore's Jurong BirdPark, is the world's largest Lory flight aviary. It envelops an existing treed valley within the Park covering an area of 3000 square metres. The aviary stands 22 metres high and affords magnificent 360 degree views across the Park. Boardwalks and suspension bridges carry visitors 12 metres above ground level for an elevated experience. The aviary construction is steel, with a stainless steel mesh surface and includes a Tree Top feeding deck, canopy suspended walks, and a themed gift shop and teahouse, which form a visitor focus for the Park.

Lory Loft is home to the Lories, which are found throughout Australasia and Papua New Guinea. A key species is the Rainbow Lorikeet, its habitat being that of the 'Top End' of Australia, ranging from lowland open forest to the dense rainforests of the highlands.

The challenge for Stuart Green, Design Director of Green & Dale Associates was to offer visitors an experience of the vast Australian "Outback" that is unique and exciting. A windmill and bushmen's hut - familiar Australian "Outback" landmarks – are incorporated into the design, evoking the character of Australia. Visitors experience a change in the Park landscape approaching the entry plaza, which is defined by its artesian windmill pump house and water tank – icons of the Australian Landscape and a focus within the Park. Paving represents the colours of the "Outback" and is flanked by a display of Australian eucalypts, flowering plants and grasses, with specimen grass trees and a baobob tree.

A twin-decked central feeding tower, suspended above the valley floor, gives visitors an opportunity to feed the birds by hand with nectar. This amazing experience heightens as throngs of lories gather, chattering loudly and filling the air with colour. It provides a unique opportunity to view these magnificent birds close-up while feeding them. The lorikeets have been specially trained by Jurong BirdPark keepers to overcome their fear of humans and to interact with visitors by feeding from the handheld nectar cups or feeding roosts. It is the ultimate "close encounter".

awards
2006, Tourism Awards, Singapore Tourism Board (STB)
TOP 10 BEST FAMILY EXPERIENCES: Feed the Lories at Jurong BirdPark

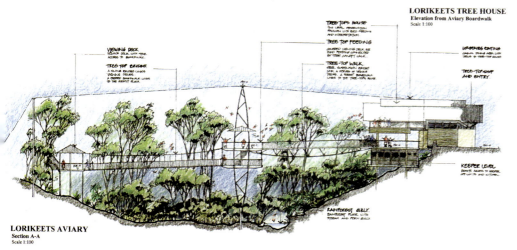

↘ Section through aviary.
↑ Lory tree top house sketch.
← Lory site plan.

↑ Cafe & Walkway suspended heigh above the valley.
↗ Lory aviary and suspension bridge.
↘↘ The suspension bridge is popular with visitors.
↘ Suspended walkways are set amongst the treed canopy of the aviary.
↓ Smaller swing bridges provide interest.

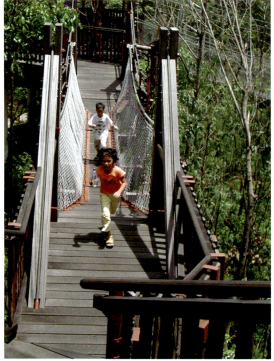

↑ Lory Loft Aviary.
↗ Baobob tree and windmill at the Lory Loft entry.
↘ Tree top cafe.
↓ Lory feeding.

client
Jurong BirdPark – Wildlife Reserves Singapore
other key consultants
Head Consultant Construction Design: PWD
Consultants Pte Singapore;
Jurong BirdPark Horticulture;
Project Management: Peter Yip.
location
Jurong, Singapore
completion
2004
photography
Stuart Green

Waitangi Park, Wellington
Wraight Athfield Landscape + Architecture Ltd.

Waitangi Park is a 4.6 hectare urban waterfront park in Wellington. It comprises the physical nexus between the City and the Harbour. In its preconstruction state the site's industrial and port surrounds relegated it to an island of struggling turf and amorphous car parking lots.

The new park constitutes complex programmatic requirements; at once a reprieve from the pressures of urban life, but concurrently a forum within which the varied dramas of urban life might be enacted. The Wraight Athfield Landscape + Architecture design seeks to challenge and reinvent the urban park within this hilly, windy, Wellington context. The park boasts a high level of mixed recreational uses augmented by environmentally sustainable design solutions. The park is circumnavigated by a permeable network of promenades drawing pedestrians from the city to the sea whilst providing a continuous foreshore link between Oriental Bay and Taranaki Wharf. The physical components of the park are amplified by woven narratives pertinent to the Wellington region, referencing both the natural and cultural heritage of the site.

The park comprises a large central field circumnavigated by a series of pathways, boardwalks, wetlands and activity spine. The park caters to a wide range of activities including children's playground, petanque, skate boarding, aerosol art spaces, rock wall climbing, ball court and other more passive recreational activities. The park's central field is defined by a linear storm water filtration system which is manifested in a series of planted wetland gardens terminating in a storage pond at the harbour's edge.

Waitangi Park's design promotes: water conservation, quality improvement of urban storm water runoff (no net increase of pollution in natural water systems), bio-diversity, and use of renewable energy, reduction of green house gases (wind / solar power) and waste reduction. All native species have been sourced within the Wellington Ecological region, thus establishing an ongoing viable easily accessed seed-source for future projects around the city.

awards
2007, Supreme Award, New Zealand Institute of Architects;
2007, Honorary mention, Torsanlorenzo International Award;
2007, Commendation, Lighting Design, NZIES.

1. Stormwater collection (offsite)
2. Sub-surface wetland
3. The stream
4. Polishing wetland
5. Storage pond
6. Stream discharge point
7. Rocky coast garden
8. Graving dock
9. Street-side promenade
10. The field
11. Children's playground
12. Petanque court
13. Skatepark
14. Canoe landing beach
15. Lobby

← Waitangi park plan.
↓ Waitangi park shortly after completion.

- 179 -

↑ Sub surface wetland section.
↗ Waitangi stream section.
↘ View towards Waka landing beach from Graving dock.
↓ Wellington rocky coast garden.
↓↓ View over entry plaza, graving dock, wetland and wind garden.

↑ Stream side promenade at night.
↗ Active edge, skate park at night.
↓ View towards playground from sub surface wetland.
↘ Waka landing broadwalk and rip rap stonework.

→ Waka pathways through shifting shoreline mound.
↘ Waitangi stream wetland.
↘↘ Graving dock gravel terraces and graving dock wetland.
↓ Waitangi stream 'holding ponds'.

↑ Activity zone, skate bowl.
→ Activity zone, skate park detail.
↓ Activity zone, street ball court.

client
Wellington Waterfront Ltd
lead consultants
Wraight Athfield Landscape + Architecture Ltd
other key consultants
Landscape Environment and Urban Design Group
– GAO – Sydney;
Ecological Engineering – Melbourne / Brisbane;
Engineers: Spencer Holmes, Wellington
location
Wellington, New Zealand
completion
2005
photography
Neil Price (Wellington City Council, unless stated)

Cairns Esplanade Skatepark, Queensland
Convic Design Pty Ltd.

The cairns skatepark is Australia's largest skatepark and is located on the popular cairns foreshore. Adjacent to an existing playground, the park layout has been derived by connecting existing access paths and the boardwalk with a series of linear skate plazas intersecting to create passive viewing spaces. In a number of key locations, bowls have been sited. The skatepark focuses both on international competitions, in line with cairns tourism focus whilst also catering for the local community.

The park has been designed as an integrated dynamic landscape, tying in with the existing beach aesthetic and creating an accessible community sports focus for the foreshore. Beach volleyball courts and a new car park that functions as an events space add to the flexibility and recreation opportunities of this major skate facility.

Trees are planted throughout the space and there are two main shade structures located around the bowls. Signage, seating and drinking fountains have also been placed strategically to maximise functionality and meet user needs.

The Cairns skatepark sets the standard in contemporary skate park provision, breaking away from traditional concrete monolithic forms to create a truly urban sporting space, reflecting the context in which it sits and providing over 2000 m^2 of diverse skate experience whilst adding visually to an already dynamic recreational coastal precinct.

↑ Overall Concept 3d render of entire park.
↗ Crowd shot of plaza during opening of park.
↓ Overall view of the completed park.

↑   BMX action shot in main bowl.
↗   Skate shot in bowl.
↗↗ BMX action shot in cradle.
↓   View of skate plaza and surrounding landscape.

↖ View of the completed small bowl area.
↑ Close up view of the cradle.
↓ Detailed view of concept 3d render of plaza.
↙ View of stairs and plaza.

client
Cairns City Council
other key consultants
Engineering of Grogan Richards and GHD
location
Cairns, Queensland, Australia
completion
2007
photography
Convic Design Pty Ltd, unless stated

Belgrave Town Park, Victoria
ASPECT Studios Pty Ltd.

ASPECT Studios undertook the design and documentation of a new town park for the major tourist village of Belgrave in the Dandenong mountains, east of Melbourne. The design of the park draws connections between the historic streetscape, the popular Puffing Billy Tourist Train and the broad mountain views afforded by its high, terraced location.

These influences worked with the "rustic" character of the town while providing a contemporary edge to its design language. The site which had extreme access and spatial constraints therefore the main boardwalk which provides access for all, forms the main feature for both the park and the township's streetscape.

↑ View from main road looking up to terrace park.
→ Design plan.
↓ Section through site.

↖ View from ramp to upper terrace.
↑ Detail of main ramp reminiscent of railway bridge.
↑↑ Construction details reminiscent of the nearby Puffing Billy Railway.
↗ Main ramp is accessible for all people.
→ Water is collected in one main design drain.
← Phragmites folly's spacing and slant suggest the force of blowing wind.

client
Shire of Yarra Ranges
other key consultants
Grogan Richards Engineers,
Martin Butcher Lighting
location
Monbulk Road, Belgrave, Victoria, Australia
completion
2005
photography
Daniel Gueli

Clewley Street Garden, Brisbane
Jeremy Ferrier Landscape Architects

awards
2005, Heritage Places (non residential), Edmund Wright Heritage Award.

OVERVIEW

The garden begins with one of those irresistibly dilapidated old Queenslanders, complete with attics, verandahs and fireplaces. We rescued our long dreamed of home from demolition and relocated it to one of Brisbane's leafy older suburbs southwest of the CBD. The new land was filled with quintessential Brisbane trees and palms including established Mango, Jacaranda, Frangipani, Fig, Poinciana, Silky Oak, Kauri and Hoop Pines as well as Alexander and Cuban Royal palms.

The garden is designed around respect for the age of the house whilst being sympathetic to the natural attributes of its new location. Functionally the garden caters for a family of five and their passion for living life outdoors. Specific requirements included expansive outdoor dining areas, open grassed play spaces, quiet contemplative pockets, a swimming pool and room for pets including chickens, ducks and guinea pigs.

DESCRIPTION

Formal and structured in concept the garden is conceived as a series of outdoor rooms –

The Arrival Courtyard - Paved with reclaimed clay bricks the Arrival Courtyard is centred on an old Cuban Royal Palm. A sculptural trellis of rusted steel frames the garden. The trellis reflects the patternation of abstracted leaf and branch structure. A gateway in the trellis forms a portal to a white mosaic sphere beyond.

The Great Lawn - The Great Lawn provides an enticing and visually soothing active recreation space. One side of the lawn is punctuated by a suite of sculptural spheres. Emerging from the shadows of the large fig at the end of this vista, three Balinese Stone Wheels on plinths provide a primeval and earthy focal point to the great lawn.

↑ Trellis door framing the mosaic sphere.
↗ Courtyard planting from the attic.

The Terrace - A giant mango tree shades an expansive terrace with built in brick barbecue which forms the hub of outdoor dining and entertaining.

The Flame Tree Forest - The Forest exists as a quiet contemplation space with two dancing seats occupying a shady position in the middle of the grove. Curved in form and entwined in their placement together they convey a sense of movement and rhythm. A marble wall forms a dramatic backdrop where mammoth slabs of marble cut and composed as a sculptural focus.

The Classical Garden - Entered through a vine covered pergola and framed by a traditional ornate timber and wire trellis the classical garden is a reflection of the architectural character of the house. The garden revolves around the Emperor's Lounge; reminiscent of the detailing of ancient Greece or Rome the seat is a playful interpretation of an antique divan.

The Cottage Garden - Massed with old fashioned but hardy flowering perennials the Cottage Garden pays homage to the type of garden historically associated with Queensland homes. The centre piece of which is a pond filled with water lilies and goldfish and highlighted by an urn of trickling water.

Good design transcends time, eschews fashion and has lasting relevance. The design demonstrates a new twist on an old subject. To complement the age and character of the house the garden is formal and traditional in structure however it is sensitively imbued with innovative and modern design elements. These elements add depth and vitality which gives the garden its individuality and soul. Elements such as the flame tree forest with marble wall and dancing seats, the sculptural trellis and the emperors lounge challenge the notion and sensibility of what a formal garden can be.

Twenty years of designing gardens for other people leads me to feel that the constraints and boundaries they bring with them make it easier than designing for oneself. There are no such constraints when designing your own garden and hence the possibilities are endless. The great danger is to try and squeeze every idea into the one space. Restraint and respect for the individuality of each space is the key to good design.

The other party to the creation of this garden is my wife, a woman of good design sense and ear for many design ideas. It is a tribute to her, whilst also a sacrifice in that she may have wanted a new bathroom however she has a marble wall and rusting trellis instead.

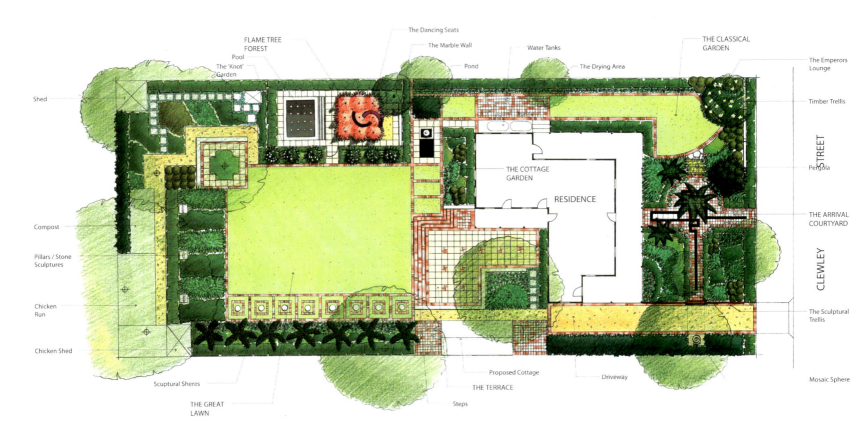

↖ Landscape plan.
↑ Stone wheel.
↗ The three stone wheels form the focal point of the garden.
→ Pond & trickling urn.
← The three stone wheels form the focal point of the garden.

↑ The forest with the pool in the foreground.
↘ Seats, walls & trunks.
↓ The forest with the pool in the background.

↑ The classical garden looking towards the arrival courtyard.
↘ Where it all began.
↓ The Emperors Lounge with the timber trellis in the background.

client
Cairns City Council
other key consultants
Engineering of Grogan Richards and GHD
location
Clewley Street Corinda Brisbane, Australia
completion
2007
photography
Imago Photography, unless stated

Habitat Wakerley, Brisbane
Jeremy Ferrier Landscape Architects

OVERVIEW

Located on the fringes of Brisbane's southern bayside suburbs the small site was in many ways unremarkable. Save for a few clumps of native trees the land was flat and featureless, it was bound by a busy road and without outlook. The area was in a flood zone requiring house pads to be filled one metre above natural ground. Had it not been for the general land shortage in Brisbane the site would likely not have been selected for development.

DESCRIPTION

The design approach focussed upon revealing and accentuating the natural landscape character. To achieve this at a site planning level a 'green zone' in the form of a linear park was created to retain these natural attributes. The park runs between the houses, commencing at the very entry to the development and culminating in a larger recreational parkland. This structure allowed for the retention of the primary concentration of existing trees.

Creating a distinctive identity within the subdivision genre was key to the detailed design. This was achieved through a series of striking elements and features which thematically tie the space together as a cohesive whole. This theme was woven around the name of the development 'Habitat', with all of the elements evolving from images of flora and fauna. To reveal the natural landscape character the colours and finishes of the built environment take on muted and earthy tones. This character is further complimented through the extensive use of Indigenous plant species.

A large recreation park was designed as the activity focus of the development and provides the opportunity for people to enjoy the natural landscape. The design of the space is driven by the playful interpretation of the Habitat theme. With the possum poles, sculpted leaves and tree trunk motif coming together in a vibrant space. These elements are brought to life when the space is filled with people making the most of the barbecue facilities, shelters, fixed play equipment and bicycle paths.

awards
2005, Heritage Places (non residential), Edmund Wright Heritage Award.

↑ The possum pole entry statement.

As a departure from the typical entry statement a family of possums sits mischievously atop a series of poles reminiscent of tree trunks to mark the front door to the development. Oversized leaves define nodal points and create casual seating opportunities. The playful forms provide visual interest and fragment the expanse of pathway. This botanical patternation of nodal points is continued in a motif of twig forms applied as a road treatment at entry points and intersections.

Acoustic buffering was a necessity due to the nature of the adjacent road. Patternation to the acoustic fence in the form of stained timber bisected by battening breaks up the expanse of fence. Wanting to ensure that local koalas retained freedom of movement a koala ladder was incorporated into the fence to provide access.

With little in the way of natural landscape character the site would potentially have developed as a bland subdivision. Design is employed as a tool to dramatically improve the lifestyle values of the development. The clever use of design elements has transformed the land into an inviting space to live in and be identified with.

Design is used to inject zest and character into the development. Design elements are employed in a playful manner to create spaces which are not only contemporary and functional but vibrant and playful. The individuality of these elements effectively makes the development stand out from the pack.

The design successfully achieves the brief of creating spaces which people wanted to spend time in, of maximising the value and appeal of the site's limited natural attributes. And in doing so encouraging many to live at Habitat, therefore fulfil the financial gaols of our client.

The design demonstrates the potential of design to take spaces in directions not previously envisaged. It illustrates that trends in design are just that and that lasting appeal comes from good design. In a climate of conservative clients it shows that taking a risk and not subscribing to the status quoi can pay off. It also reminds us that playfulness and a sense of humour and fun are valuable commodities in our built environment.

©Jeremy Ferrier

↑ The entry statement looking across the leaf motif.
↗ Leaf panel.
↗↗ Leaf nodal point.
↘↘ BBQ seating area shaped in the image of a leaf.
↘ The mounded play area and adventure path with possum poles.
↓ The "green zone" linear park.

↖ 'Twig' pattern in roadway.
↑ Possum sculpture.
↓ The cheeky possum.
← The beginning of the "Green Zone" linear park.

client
Cairns City Council
other key consultants
Engineering of Grogan Richards and GHD
location
Cairns, Queensland, Australia
completion
2007
photography
Imago Photography, unless stated

Manukau City Council Cultural Performance Garden 2006, Manurewa
Chow:Hill Architects Ltd.

This year's Manukau City Council exhibition garden builds on the 'performance garden' theme established at the Ellerslie Flower Show for the first time in 2005. The focus of the garden is to celebrate the rich cultural identity of Manukau City, and in particular its arts and culture.

The design aims to excite people about the potential for Manukau City, focusing on the cultures of the South Pacific, including Maori and New Zealand. The garden was required to push the boundaries of the traditional performance space, and be reinforced by creative and vibrant planting of the highest quality.

The theme
Manukau City is a proud melting pot of over 165 ethnic groups, with a vibrant arts and culture scene largely based around the fusion between the Pacific Rim cultures with the traditional 'Kiwi' way of life. This fusion is underpinned by the strong connections to the land of the Maori people. The Maori world view has influenced both the early European immigrants and the later arrivals from the Pacific Rim and beyond. This layering of cultures has created a unique 'Kiwi' character that is strongly evident in Manukau today.

The 2006 concept reflects New Zealand's strong links to the land, illustrated by the transition from natural to built elements across the site. Natural planting elements rise and twist out of the ground before becoming solidified, ordered and structured in the sculptured concrete form of the stage. The physical forms in the garden are derived from traditional weaving patterns, with loose natural strands looping and crossing each other before solidifying in the form of a wrapped woven basket that encloses the stage structure.

South Pacific cultures are represented in the garden through three large carved timber forms inspired by the 'Moai' of Easter Island, carved by recognised sculptor Fatu Feu'u. These bright red sculptures rise out of the subtropical planting, and strengthen

awards
2006 Silver Award, Ellerslie Flower Show

the strong complementary colour palette of the planting.

The stage itself is created as a series of four bound flax strands, one set above the others as if being finally woven in to complete the construction. The routed grooves reflect the grid traditionally created by stripping the flax strands back with a sharp tool.

The stage form is cantilevered out over a sculpted landform and is set above the audience's eye line to allow for optimum viewing. Dense subtropical planting to both sides helps to enclose the stage and lead the eye towards the performances.

While the public were excluded from exhibition gardens this year, the performers were encouraged to interact with the garden, as a number of sculptural drums are set amongst the planting. Together with the offset heights on the stage, this resulted in dynamic and varied performances.

The planting is a bold mix of South Pacific and native planting - a fusion mirroring the makeup of the City's population.

Plants have been sourced from the South Pacific only, and adhere to a strict red, green and black colour combination, to support the brightly coloured Moai. The intent was to create a lush backdrop for the stage, reflective of the subtropical climate that Manukau enjoys. Unusual planting combinations are played up, to encourage visitors to consider options that are 'outside the square' in their own planting.

The planting has been strengthened by the inclusion of decorative botanical patterning to a number of the built elements, including the screening panels and drums. These motifs, based around the flowers of the South Pacific combine with the decorative and lush planting to offset and contrast the unapologetically hard built form of the stage.

↑ Bands of planting ran over and under each other on their way to the stage.
↓ Red, black and green were the dominant colours for the garden reflecting the vibrancy of the Manukau culture.

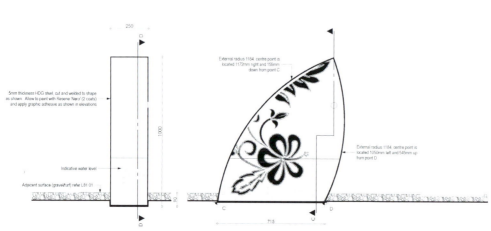

← The backing panels for the garden featured 'Frangipanni' imagery to soften their appearance.

↖ Dense subtropical planting framed each side of the stage.

↑ Red Fatu Feu'u 'Moai' rise out of the planting as if watching the audience.

↓ Ply and bamboo drums were used by the performers to enliven the garden.

↙ The South Pacific 'Frangipanni' motif was chosen to 'soften' the hard elements.

- ↖ Initial concept plan, showing the strong colour themes.
- ↙ The layering created by the weaving process was explored to inspire the built form.
- ↙↙ Traditional weaving processes influenced the stage form and garden layout.

client
Manukau City Council
other key consultants
Structural: Holmes Consulting;
Artists: Fatu Feu'u and Isa Staron-Tutugoro;
Quantity Surveying: Maltby's.
location
2006 Ellerslie Flower Show, Manurewa, Auckland
completion
2006
photography
Dave Little and Penny Kerr

Carnegie Library Play Space: The Bookworms, Victoria
FORMium / Mark McWha Landscape Architects

DESIGN OVERVIEW
The Carnegie Library Play Space is intended as a colourful contemporary urban vignette play environment, to be enjoyed by children of all abilities, and the local community as a whole. The library site context is 'played-up' with the use of the 'Glen Eira Bookworm' character as a key play element. Three individual sculptural bookworm elements intertwine over book stacks, to offer an innovative play experience, giving an opportunity to fully explore the 'play instinct' in children.

THE BOOKWORMS
Each of the scrambling sculptural bookworms provides children of all age groups with opportunities for imaginative play. These are thematically designed and are named as 'Musical Bookworm', 'Glow Bookworm' and 'Clamber Bookworm'.

Both musical and clamber worms are covered with rubber softfall, with distinctive theme colours. Play elements like drums, climbing studs, skeleton hoops and fins are articulated as part of their sculptural form. These elements act as scales and protrusions over the worms anatomical forms. The book stacks act as seating platforms or stages and enable children to reach the head of the worm. The glow bookworm is fabricated of translucent fibre reinforced glass, which is lit from within, and glows bright as the night falls.

The shapes are recognisable, but leave room for interpretation, and imagination. They can be used in a variety of ways: as scramble/agility devices; for climbing and hiding; to discover nooks; for music; and as gathering and seating mounds. Each segments of glow bookworm are arranged with gaps making the space permeable for kids to run around, to hide and to discover. There are ramped routes in-and-around the play area for exploring by wheelchair and with pram.

The paving around the sculptures is covered with rubberised softfall, in a colourful

awards
2006 Innovation in Design of Playground Elements, Kidsafe National Playground Design Award;
2006 PRAV Award, Playgrounds and Recreation Association of Victoria.

↑ Overall view.
↓ Playground plan and elevation.

chequerboard pattern allowing children to play a variety of 'floor' games. The pattern is intended to contrast dramatically with the 'organic' forms of the worms.

THE INTERACTIVE BOOKWORM TOTEMS

A range of interactive metal sculptural bookworm totems are located at one end of playspace. They have LED lights for eyes, which light up in changing colours when their given names are spelled out on an interactive keyboard. Buttons of the keyboard are arranged like a laptop keyboard with a display screen. These totems are also touch sensitive, when hugged, cuddled or pampered, they amuse and respond back with a soft laughing / giggling sound, with lit up eyes in different colours. One of the sculptural totem recites stories and nursery rhymes.

THE MURAL WALL AND STAGE

A special feature of the space is the rear book leaf shaped mural wall. Two of the panels are set-aside as art walls for local community groups, schools etc. It is intended that the works will be 'fleeting', to be re-worked by a group or a new young local 'artist', on a monthly basis.

In front of the book leaf shaped mural wall is a raised platform, as performance stage. There is provision for audiovisual connections. The crawling worms act as seating mounds to view performances. Other local 'symbols' and signage information are recorded on the wall panels, with key words depicting local symbols – indigenous vegetation, local history, interpretation of Koori Place names, etc. Braille, pictographs and hand signage are integrated into these elements.

This playful environment, within this local bustling urban niche space provides children with ways to express their creative play 'urges', and to provide opportunities for imaginative and interactive play, and to foster a 'free play' environment.

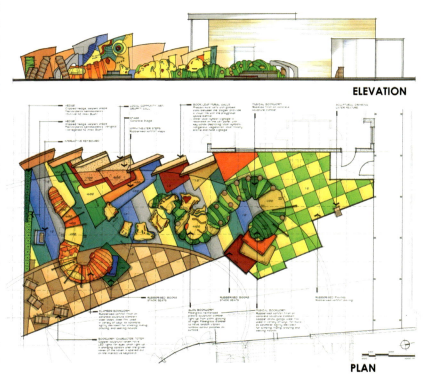

↑ Climber bookworm.
↗ Musical bookworm.
↓ Book leaf shaped mural wall and stage.

↑ Interactive bookworm totems.
↘↘ Bookworm fountain.
↘ Glow bookworm at night.
↓ Glow bookworm.

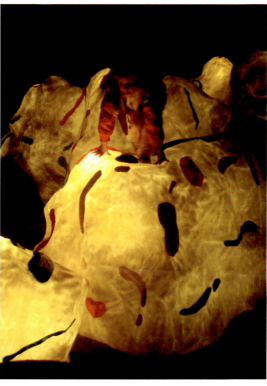

client
Glen Eira City Council
other key consultants
Landscape Contractor: Living Landscape
location
Carnegie Library, Shepparson Street, Carnegie, Victoria, Australia
completion
2006 / 2007
photography
Suresh Shiva & Mark McWha

Residential

Glentrees Condominium, Singapore
ICN Design International

awards
2005/6, Gold (High Density Housing), Singapore Institute of Landscape Architects (SILA), Professional Design Awards;
2006, Urban Land Institute Awards for Excellence: Asia Pacific.

The site is bounded on one side by the mainline railway, and on another by a school. This prompts the architecture to face inwards with the 5 balconied storeys stepping progressively backwards to form a "valley garden" in the centre. Since the basement car park will cover the entire site area, the gardens are all on roof decks with limited loading capacity. The gardens are designed to be naturalised in style, and shady with an open and airy feel, as one would find in a light woodland.

The landscape focuses on the creation of usable space and attractive views from all of the rooms at all levels. The stepping back of the balconies brings greenery up the side of the buildings, letting in abundant light and fresh air. For the creation of substantial greenery, the provision of deep soil bodies for trees is a priority, and much work has been done to achieve the hidden structure needed to achieve maximum planting. The brief calls for a 50m lap pool which has been successfully integrated with a substantial leisure pool and kids "wet play" area, while still providing plenty of sundeck and lounging areas. The tight outer boundary means that fire-engine access has to pass through the central gardens but it is cleverly concealed within the planting design.

The main gardens are divided into character areas to provide a sense of variety and distinction between the different residential blocks. The wider

spaces have been set out as usable gardens where families can gather and children can run around freely. The Misty Rock Garden is one such space, where there is a water play rocky stream surrounded by shady trees and flowering shrubs.

The narrow spaces are walkways leading from one part of the site to another, such as the Meadow Valley, a garden of grasses and meandering paths where hidden water-springs provide a cooling sound.

In the central gardens there are lily ponds with timber bridges meandering through drifts of exotic waterside planting.

The Club House and Gymnasium are located at the basement facing out into an attractive landscape courtyard which is open to the upper gardens as a series of cascading terraces, abundantly planted with rich tropical plants. Within the courtyard are clear pools with large Koi fish and fern planters.

The main entrance forms an archway leading into the gardens, and this has a distinctly modern look with stone and water features surrounded by leafy bamboos. The Jacuzzi area is also of bamboo character where residents can relax in a quiet and private corner under the shade of tropical foliage.

↑ Aerial view of main pool.
↘ Masterplan.

- ↖ The main pool environmental deck.
- ↑ Wet lounger alcove
- ↓ Car park access emerges through pool.
- ← Timber causeway diguises a sub-structure step and separates the main pool from the children's pool.
- ↙ The main pool environmental deck.

← The lily pond with meandering timber bridges passing through drifts of waterside plants.
→ The Misty Rock Garden.
↘ Soft landscape treatment to fire engine access paths into the podium deck.
↓ The Misty Rock garden with interactive water play.
↙ The lily pond with meandering timber bridges passing through drifts of waterside plants.
↙↙ The Jaccuzzi with sitting deck and tropical planting enclosure.

client
Leonie Court Private Limited (A subsidiary of Capital Land)
other key consultants
Architect: MKPL
location
Mount Sinai, off Holland Road, Singapore
completion
Oct, 2005
photography
Henry Steed

Southport Central, Queensland
Place Design Group

Seamlessly uniting residential, commercial and retail space, the three towers of Southport Central will be a striking tribute to a new direction in the evolution of one of the Gold Coast's most established central precincts.

Currently the largest mixed use development under construction in Australia, Southport Central is a $700 million development that is leading the reinvention of Southport.

Between the natural confines of the broadwater and mountainous hinterland, Southport Central expresses the Gold Coast's dynamic global identity through timeless design.

Wake up to panoramic views of the Broadwater and ocean beyond, river or hinterland.
Relax at the Garden Gallery – an exclusive resort-style retreat with an oasis of fountains, lush tropical landscaping, pools, gym and barbeque entertainment areas – just for residents and their guests.

Enjoy the vibrance and convenience of Central Fountains, Southport Central's own retail precinct with boutique shopping and cosmopolitan cafes and restaurants surrounded by striking water features.

↓ Ground level urban landscape waterfeatures and gardens.

← Ground level urban landscape view through axis.
↓ Urban art seat and light element.

← Aerial view of private tower gardens.
↑ Resort pool and sun deck.
↘ Sheer decent waterfeatures and outdoor shower.
↓ Resort pool waterfeature.

client
Raptis Group
other key consultants
Architect: Archidiom Design;
Engineer: Connell Wagner;
Construction: Rapcivic
location
Southport, Queensland, Australia
completion
On-going
photography
Denise Yates

M Central, Sydney
360° Landscape Architecture

awards
2006 Australian Timber Design Awards
  (Commendation)

ROOFTOP LANDSCAPE

Scope of work – concept design to project delivery for a 3,000m² communal rooftop landscape spanning the rooftops of the Goldsborough Mort & Pitt, Son & Badgery Woolstores in Pyrmont, Sydney. The scope of work also included the design of private courtyards to 19 penthouse apartments, as well as public domain works at street level. The client's brief was general, calling for the creation of a landscape that wasn't a 'typical rooftop with a swimming pool'.

Intent & Concept

The response to limited outdoor private space due to heritage issues was to create an unexpected rooftop landscape, an island in the sky, a green roof that's accessible and functional for all residents and that makes a positive ecological contribution to the urban environment.

The design process centred on the experiential qualities of floating through a landscape, dominated by a grassland, vivid with colour and movement that leads to interesting and diverse functional areas, where each space enables residents to choose how they interact.

The communal landscape is split over levels 6 & 7 and caters to approximately 400 residents living on the 7 floors. With large areas of open space in parks and playing fields in nearby Wentworth Park and Glebe, the design intent was to provide an alternative experience which overlays the expansive rooftop space and its CBD and district views, with a sense of intimacy in the immediate landscape.

Rather than seek to maximize the rooftop area that residents could access, the intent focused on how it would be used and experienced in niche spaces. It was also important to retain the sense of being on a rooftop, and at times to feel its exposure, with the provision of protected and shaded spaces to offer refuge, privacy and a general sense of being immersed in an extensive and richly planted landscape.

↑ View northwest over split level to Blackwattle Bay and beyond.

The key landscape elements that emerged from the design intent are derived from the raised timber deck paths which 'float' over the landscape, through an expansive native grassland and lead to a variety of recreation opportunities. These include both private and communal spaces:

- secret lawns;
- a children's softfall play area;
- bbq facilities;
- an entertaining deck under a sculptural arbor cloaked in flowering climbers,
- shaded bench seats adjacent a painted landscape of recycled concrete and terracotta mulches; and
- a granite water wall and stainless steel water rill that interplays with the grasses and leads to an ornamental pond.

Special Factors

Unique in scale in Sydney's CBD, the rooftop landscape is a vibrant communal recreation space and a local precedent for the sustainable and ecological opportunities for rooftop developments in Australia.

The former woolstores had been converted into a 7 storey public carpark including parking on the exposed concrete roof. There were significant challenges in converting a former carpark into a communal rooftop park, of a scale that is unique in Sydney's CBD.

Site specific responses include:

- Harsh, exposed and dramatic site conditions - selection of appropriate mix of hardy native and exotic plant species.
- Protection of residents views from the adjacent Goldsborough Mort residences which limited the ability to provide shade and privacy to Level 6 of the rooftop – the creation of a climber clad arbour to the split level provides shade and privacy, an adjacent waterwall, rill and pond helps cool the space, a single Dracaena draco provides shade amongst the grasses, and lying down in the pockets of turf amongst grasses provides privacy and a sense of intimacy.
- The engineering response to support the rooftop planting comprised a grid of upturned beams – a maximum soil depth of 300mm was permitted and specimen trees were limited to being placed over columns below. Foam packing was implemented between the upturned beams to minimise loading. Appropriate succulents, grasses and hardy coastal plant species were selected for the soil depth, and the level 3 water restrictions.

M Central Landscape Concept Plan HARRIS STREET

← Intimate lawn pockets immersed in the field of native grasses.
↑ Under the arbour, down by the water wall.
↓ Level 7 – recycled decorative mulches (terracotta and concrete), timber path and shade tree planters adjacent childrens' softfall play area.
↙↙ Level 7 – recycled decorative mulches (terracotta and concrete), timber path and shade tree planters leading to play area.
↙ Concept Plan.

← Dracaena draco in turf plinth.
↘ Building - Harris Street Entry.
↓ Timber pedestrian bridges, paths and privacy screens.
↓↓ Water wall – granite, bluestone and stainless steel.
↙ Timber path through grasses.

client
The Hayson Group
other key consultants
Architects: Marchese + Partners, Dale Jones Evans
location
Ultimo, Sydney, Australia
photography
John Gollings, unless stated

Vajra Villas, Ubud Bali
Sheils Flynn Ltd.

This small cluster of villas is set within a stunning landscape of sawah and steep valley slopes on the edge of a Balinese village. It is designed for a client who is seeking the perfect meditation retreat and the buildings are carefully sited so that they are integrated within the landscape, affording a sequence of beautiful composed views without intrusion. The site of each villa is aligned to fit with the valley's natural contours and the buildings are tucked close to tracts of existing mature woodland leaving the extensive local sawah untouched. The traditional sawah is maintained by local farmers who keep a proportion of the produce.

From the enclosed parking area, visitors enter a group of small villas and courtyard before passing through a striking screen wall entrance onto a boardwalk across the sawah. This open causeway is designed to follow the existing geometry of the sawah and there are stunning uninterrupted views to the padi to the south and a group of ornate village temples to the north. At the end of the boardwalk, a small square jetty acts as a gateway to the first villa.

The living spaces are arranged around a sequence of decks, pools and gardens which are designed to provide spaces for meeting, eating and talking as well as for quiet contemplation. The rooms are designed in conjunction with the landscape with stunning framed views at every turn. There are many surprises: even the bathrooms have tiny windows focusing on the padi beyond. The pace of life slows in this open plan environment of water, lush vegetation, stepping stones and sculpture. The villas step gradually down the valley side so the river is a constant backdrop in views from the decks and gardens.

Indigenous plant material is used throughout and the interface between interior and exterior is deliberately blurred. Sheils Flynn worked closely with our client, PT Vajra, to design and construct an intimate and exquisitely detailed Balinese landscape which extends from within the complex of buildings to embrace the wider environs.

↗ Illustrative Masterplan.
↘ Terrace beside the sawah.
↓ Entrance to the villa complex from the car park.

← The villas are tucked against the valley sides so that the local sawah is conserved.
↙ Path leading to the main villa.
↙↙ Poolside planting.

↑ Stepping stones to bedroom pavilion.
↗ Deck with view to river valley.
↓ Outdoor dining area.

client
PT Vajra.
other key consultants
PT Grounds Kent Arsitek Indonesia;
CV Catur Mitra Utama;
David Hutchinson HST architects.
location
Ubud, Bali, Indonesia
photography
Sheils Flynn

Tatham Residence, Queenstown
Morgan+Pollard Associates Queenstown

This house is located in the rural part of the Wakatipu Basin. The new owners of the dwelling have carried out modifications and extensions to suit their needs. The previously rudimentary landscape was in need of a significant upgrade.

The brief was to create a contemporary and formal landscape/ garden setting for the extended building with various outdoor living options – while respecting the rural setting. The extended landscape was to be strongly connected to the garden and provide for an interesting and generous approach to the house.

Design
Vegetation:
A simple palette of deciduous trees was selected in accordance with the already established species. Many single trees, previously planted in a "gardenesque" fashion were removed and a new structure created. The pond and wetland areas (absorbing and treating large amounts of stormwater runoff from driveway and neighbouring land) were planted with adequate local indigenous plants. We dared to experiment with transplanting mature (1.5m tall), potentially century-old Carex secta plants that had to be removed from another site. Success was sweet! After one vegetation period, the plants started to thrive and the Paradise ducks loved it!

The palette of plants in the garden was designed to reflect the hot, dry setting within the basin, while the courtyard and borders on the south side provided the opportunity to use shade-loving plants.

Hard Elements:
Concrete, gravel, steel, schist and Macrocarpa timber were used in their raw, natural forms. In the fire place, plastered walls to match elements of the house played the major role.

↑ The wetland and pond receive and clean the stormwater while providing an idyllic foreground for the arrival experience..
↓ The imposing fireplace matches the dimensions of the chimney at the opposite end of the house and encloses the eastern outdoor area.

Pond:
The centerpiece of the arrival experience. The narrow, widening wetland area – being the recipient of stormwater run-off – "guides" the visitor along the driveway towards the house. Apart from the transplanting of the Carex secta, the design and construction of the pond itself was somewhat experimental. This was the first pond sealed with Geosynthetic Clay Liner (GCL) in the southern South Island. The result was outstandingly positive in respect to construction, ecological balance and appearance.

House Garden:
Strong, architectural lines attempt to fulfill the brief. However, where suitable, the lines are breached with rather lush vegetation "spilling over the edges". Pergola and fireplace extend the architecture out into the landscape and pick up themes from the original building.

Entrance:
The narrow throat did not allow for much creativity but discussions with the neighbour allowed for some common treatment of this area. A simple wooden gate provides for enclosure while maintaining a low-key appearance.

↑ The Macrocarpa timber pergola and the structural Buxus blocks.
↓ The pond and wetland looking towards the north-west.

↑ Pond margin planting incorporates the unique Carex secta - a New Zealand sedge growing a trunk".
↘↘ The entrance lines up with the magnificent Remarkables mountain range.
↘ The southern courtyard contains lush structural plants such as ferns and Macleya.
↓ Paving detail: schist stone strips structuring concrete and gravel surfaces.

client
P Tatham
other key consultants
Landscape Construction: GreenBelt Ltd ·
 Morgan+Pollard Queenstown Ltd;
Irrigation Design: Water Control Solutions Ltd;
Fireplace and Pergola: Roy Bagley Builder
location
Queenstown, New Zealand
completion
2004

Edgar Landscape, Queenstown
Morgan+Pollard Associates Queenstown

The site is located on the sunny Kelvin Heights Peninsula in Queenstown. It comprises three sections amalgamated to one lot on the shores of Frankton Arm of Lake Wakatipu. The original holiday home of the family had been here for 35 years and was relocated directly across the lake where it now looks back "home" with envy.

The new house was designed and constructed in several phases over a period of about 3 years. Landscape construction followed progress in three separate stages. Stage 1 (roadside planting) was completed in autumn 2003; stage 2 (lakeside construction and planting) was completed in autumn 2004 and stage 3 (entrance courtyard and water feature) finalised the project in November 2004. Stage 4 is currently in progress and comprises design and construction of a new jetty.

Much emphasis was placed on creating a cohesive landscape between the site, the foreshore and walkway reserve and the road reserve. Respectful treatment of the public spaces was deemed necessary to achieve the best possible outcome for all parties – maximum separation, public access and usability as well as realistic management practice.

The brief was simple and contained three broad criteria: design to be contemporary and harmonious with the architecture; integrate public spaces; achieve adequate privacy while maintaining views and vistas.

Design
Vegetation:
The (almost) exclusive use of indigenous species was long debated with the clients, but finally agreed. Obviously, the simplicity of the architecture, the size of the site and the generosity of the setting required a limited palette. After testing a rather puristic, ecologically based approach, we felt that the inclusion of some cultivars and

awards
2006, Gold awards for design, hard landscape construction, soft landscape construction and landscape management, the New Zealand Institute of Landscape Architects and the Landscape Industries Association of New Zealand.

← The steep entrance driveway is dissected by the alpine creek and the "ford" feature.
↓ The alpine creek and rock features.

varieties was justified to achieve the design outcome desired.

Hard Elements:
Natural, raw materials were selected and used in their simplest form. Lake gravels and crusher dust, hardwood and local schist together with concrete were in fact the only materials altogether. Obviously, the water feature involved the use of complex construction methods and materials.

Roadside:
Along the busy local distributor road, the key was the creation of good separation and visual screening. Neighbours above the site were anxious about retention of their lakeviews and careful design of a sustainable screen planting was required.

Lakeside:
Original inspiration was the terraced landform of the ancient, narrow beach terraces. Bands of vegetation followed these terraces. These bands were then intersected with patterns of different textures created by paths and planting. Sculptures were included in a co-operative way between clients, artists and landscape architects.

Entrance Courtyard:
Difficult access! The steep driveway, the tennis court and the forecourt proved to be a challenge. The heart of the entrance experience was to be the waterfall. Because the place has been home to a crib for many years, the continuation of this feeling played a role – albeit in a symbolic way! The "ford", the mountain stream and the copse of red beech will over time work together.

↑ The sculpture named "tussock" provides a striking contrast to the serene lakeside scene while blending with forms of the vegetation.
↓ Bands of local indigenous vegetation link architecture and natural environment – in spring.

↑ The constructed, naturalistic alpine creek is the dominant feature in the entrance and arrival area providing movement, sound and focus.
↓ Bands of local indigenous vegetation link architecture and natural environment – in autumn with the native toe toe grass in flower.
↘ Purple NZ flax and Gossamer Grass.

client
J + E Edgar
other key consultants
Sculpture: Kon Dimopoulos;
Landscape Construction: GreenBelt Ltd ·
  Morgan+Pollard Queenstown Ltd;
Irrigation Design: Water Control Solutions Ltd;
Architecture: Fearon Hay Architects Ltd;
Driveway Concrete: Naylor Love Central.
location
Queenstown, New Zealand
completion
2004

Hocking Place Bushtop, Adelaide
Fifth Creek Studio

The concept of the Australian "bush" is brought into the city with this green rooftop, or bushtop, that mimics the endemic ecosystems of the original landscape of the city of Adelaide. The Hocking Place bushtop provides a domestic-scale green oasis with site-specific biodiversity for a multi-storey residential building in the heart of the city. It serves as an aerial backyard for the building's residents, and as one stepping stone habitat in a potential city-wide network of bushtops. This bushtop was designed as a retro-fit to the newly completed building, and was specially designed to suit the existing structural requirements. The bushtop achieves one twentieth of a carbon credit, therefore countering the building's consumption and emission of CO_2s.

Particular fauna species have been targeted by planting selected native grasses and sedges to provide a food source for known species of small birds that were once common in the Adelaide Plains, and the flowering plants will attract butterflies and other insects. A bat box has been installed to attract micro-bats, useful in the control of mosquitoes and flying ants.

This bushtop is an example of an accessible intensive green roof, combining animal and insect habitat with passive recreational access by the building's residents. Seating has been provided under a pergola for residents to take in the view over the city and to enjoy the year round colourful display of native plantings. The design maximises this relatively small space with pathways between pebble mulched planting beds, and mounding providing height variation and micro environments for specialised species.

This 78 m² ecologically focused rooftop landscape makes a strong statement in a direction that, while relatively new in Australia, is much needed in all our built-up urban centres, and demonstrates what can occur instead of the traditional paved roof terrace.

awards
2007, Residential Award for Landscape, Australian Institute of Landscape Architects SA;
2007, Special Citation – Future Directions, Australian Institute of Landscape Architects SA

↑ Providing habitats.
↗ Landscape architect installing bat box.
↗↗ Future shade by native climber.
→ Grasses dry off in summer.

↑ Mounding for height variation.
↗ Wildlife attractive native plants.
↗↗ Native grasses and sedges.
↓ Landscape architect showing resident how to cut back grasses.

↑ View over Adelaide.
↘ Installing rooftop landscape.
↓ Deep pebble mulch.

client
Multi Agency Community Housing Association
other key consultants
Architect: Flightpath Architects
location
Adelaide, South Australia, Australia
completion
2006
photography
Fifth Creek Studio

Company Profile

360° Landscape Architecture
Level 5 68 Wentworth Ave Surry Hills NSW 2010,
Australia
T: +612 9212 2204   F: +612 9212 2256
360@360.net.au
www.360.net.au
Daniel Baffsky AAILA, Principal

ASPECT Studios Pty Ltd.
Head Office (Melbourne) -
Level 1, 30-32 Easey Street, Collingwood,
Victoria, Australia, 3066
T: + 61 3 9417 6844   F: +61 3 9417 6855
info@aspect.net.au
www.aspect.net.au
Chris Razzell, National Director

Sydney - Studio 61, Level 6,
61 Marlborough Street, Surry Hills,
New South Wales, Australia, 2010
T: + 61 2 9699 7182   F: +61 2 9699 7192
aspectsydney@aspect.net.au

Queensland - 172 Scarborough Street, Southport, Queensland,
Australia, 4215
T: + 61 7 5503 0800   F: +61 7 5503 0877
aspectqld@aspect.net.au

China Head Office
Floor 19, Unit A, Wenjin Tower, No.23,Tianbei No.1 Road, Luohu District,
Shenzhen, 518020 China
T: + 86 0755 2550 8205   F: +86 0755 2550 8207
info@aspect.net.au
David He Xiao, China Director
M: +86 13825289603

Chow:Hill Architects Ltd.
PO Box 109169, Newmarket,
Auckland 1149, New Zealand
T: +64 9 522 6489   F: +64 9 522 6461
bridgit@chowhill.co.nz
www.chowhill.co.nz
Bridgit Diprose

3600 is a studio-based landscape architectural practice that has been involved in significant projects for public, institutional and private clients, locally, regionally and internationally, since 2001. We provide a collaborative consultancy committed to sustainable social, cultural and environmental outcomes, responding equally to the essence of the site and the vision for the project.

The practice has developed strong interdisciplinary relationships with award-winning architects, artists, engineers, developers and councils. Within these collaborations, we have a noted reputation for sensitivity to the local character, expressed by spaces, materials, forms, details and planting designs which respect, respond to, and embellish the intrinsic values of the site.

Our key members have multiple interdisciplinary qualifications and our team is widely experienced, both locally and abroad, in all aspects of landscape architecture including masterplanning, urban design, horticulture and ecology.

Our collaborative studio framework has attracted a diverse portfolio of commissions from contemporary to ecological and heritage landscapes and therein, we have delivered a wide range of successful design solutions over a wide range of projects. We apply a rigorous process of professional and philosophical research and consultation before undertaking each commission. Each project is directly overseen by the principal with particular attention to producing original, beautiful and meaningful concepts, communicated by thorough and high-quality documentation, and with a proven commitment to meeting project budgets and programmes.

Aspect is a group of design studios united through a philosophical ethos that delivers innovative, leading-edge landscape architecture and urban design, in both Australia and internationally. Since 1993 Aspect has grown on the strength of its reputation for design-led solutions and is recognised as a design office with a strong capability to deliver innovative and sustainable urban and regional projects. As a group, Aspect has seen its projects realized with award-winning results throughout Australia, Asia and the Middle East.

Aspect is founded across the three eastern states of Australia. The Melbourne practice was established in 1993, Sydney in 1997 and SE Queensland and Aspect Digital in 2003. Aspect commenced international projects in 2000 and began work in China in 2003. Our head office in China is located in Shenzhen and partner offices are located in Beijing and Shanghai.

A similar philosophy ties the practices together, responding to the local forces and character of their regions. Our portfolio of projects demonstrates a diversity and breadth of work, within Australia and internationally. This characterizes Aspect's commitment to the public realm and the broader environment.

Aspect has received peer recognition through professional awards, reviews in prominent journals and winning national and international design competitions. The Directors of Aspect are respected professionals in Australia, having lectured at universities throughout the world. They are involved with professional institutes and consult with significant government agencies in Australia and China. Aspects work ethics revolves around the following criteria:
-        Quality
-        Sustainability
-        Contemporary Approach
-        Diversity
-        Design Process
-        Project Delivery

Leadership in Total Design
Chow:Hill was established in 1992 and has three offices throughout New Zealand. With a staff of over 80, the company focuses on providing leadership in strategic planning, architecture, urban design, interior design, landscape architecture and design management.

Coe Design Landscape Architecture
Beach Studio, The Cottage, Helen Lane,
Weymouth, Dorset DT4 8AX, UK
T: +44 (0) 1305 770 666   F: +44 (0) 1305 780 022
design@coe-design.co.uk
www.coe-design.co.uk
Jennifer Coe (Principal)

1st Floor, 66 Marylebone High Street,
London W1V 5JF, UK
T: +44 (0) 20 7486 5738   F: +44 (0) 20 7486 5738
mail@coe-design.co.uk

Convic Design Pty Ltd.
Un it 13, 46-50 Regent Street, Richmond, Victoria, Australia
T: +61 3-9486-9899   F: +61 3-9486-9088
aaron@convicdesign.com
www.convic.com
Aaron Wallis

EDAW, Inc.
150 Chestnut Street, San Francisco, CA 94111 USA
T: +1 415 955 2800   F: +1 415 955 788 4875
todd.kohli@edaw.com
www.edaw.com
Todd Kohli, Landscape Architect

Coe Design Landscape Architecture are committed to innovative and imaginative contemporary landscape architecture. We specialise in modern design, to create notable landscapes and have a particular concern for expressing and enhancing the quality of a specific landscape.

We specialise in work in the city, urban design, parks, and have expertise in urban design, site planning, urban regeneration, masterplans, modern landscapes in historic settings and landscapes that complement notable architecture.

Much of our work focuses on sustainability and environmental issues; we provide a comprehensive range of services that provide the client with scope to create unique places that also address concerns about creating wildlife habitat, water and energy conservation, micro climates, plant and materials resourcing and the carbon footprint of the scheme.

The British Embassy in Sana'a, Yemen has recently won an Emirate Glass Leaf 2007 award at a recent ceremony in London in the 'Best Environmentally Sustainable Project of the Year' category. The landscaped grounds of the embassy extensively used water conservation methods, local materials and local building techniques and an on-site nursery to grow on native species, tolerant to drought and wind.

We have worked in collaboration with many leading architects and Engineers, as part of a multi-disciplinary team in the creation of modern Architecture and its settings for major public buildings in UK and European cities.

Convic Design is an international award winning design practice that contains a diverse mix of athletes and professionally qualified designers who work collaboratively on the like minded goal of developing the most innovative, integrated design solutions for clients around the world.

Convic Design has designed over 250 skate & BMX parks worldwide and also has significant experience in all facets of Landscape Architecture including urban design, master planning for active & teenage recreation, parks & recreation trails and youth inclusive public space.

When engaged collaboratively the design & construction arms of Convic work as a team so that the transition from design to construction implementation is smooth & ensures value for money, overall design integrity & construction quality.

This collaboration has resulted in the construction of more skate facilities than any other company world wide and highlights include the Worlds largest skatepark, the SMP facility in Shanghai China, Cairns skatepark, the single largest skatepark in Australia and recently the design of Singapore's national skate facility.

For more than 65 years, EDAW's collaborative approach to landscape architecture, planning/urban design, environmental planning, and economics has shaped sustainable environments across the globe. EDAW is consistently ranked among the world's leading design firms with over 1600 professionals working from a network of 35 offices worldwide, EDAW's multidisciplinary team is both broad and specialized. We measure project success by a sustainable environmental, economic and social "triple bottom line," with the goal to enhance and sustain the world's built, natural and social environments.

Fifth Creek Studio
P. O. Box 515, Montacute, South Australia 5134
Australia
T: +61 8 8390 2292 F: +61 8 8390 2323
fifthcreek@ozemail.com.au
Graeme Hopkins
Christine Goodwin

FORM*ium* Pty LTD ,
Mark McWha Landscape Architects
23 Budd Street, Collingwood 3066, Australia
T: +61 3-9416-1755   F: +61 3-9416-0508
mcwha@interdomain.net.au
Mark McWha, Suresh Shiva

Green & Dale Associates
226 Kerr Street, Fitzroy, Victoria 3065, Australia
T: +61 3-9417-5322   F: +61 3-9417-5204
sgreen@greenanddale.com.au
greenanddale.com.au
Stuart Green

Graeme Hopkins and Christine Goodwin, the directors of Fifth Creek Studio (FCS), have worked together for over 20 years, specialising in landscape, urban design and public art projects in rural communities throughout Australia. FCS projects include tourist resorts, public open space master planning and design, parklands and recreational facilities, heritage gardens and cemeteries conservation, and sustainable wetland, lakes and riverfront development. FCS projects have won state and national awards for architecture, landscape architecture, urban design and heritage conservation.

In recent years FCS has focused on environmental sustainability, including water conservation and reuse, protection and re-establishment of native fauna habitats, and use of natural systems for shading and other environmental controls. These principles are carried through all levels of design, from private residences to broad scale open space planning and design. In particular, this approach has been directed to the design of bushtop landscapes where the green roof concept is expanded to incorporate specific habitats for animals, reptiles and insects.

In 2006 a Churchill Memorial Fellowship enabled Graeme Hopkins to visit and research green roofs and living walls in North America, Japan, Singapore and Malaysia. FCS is conducting research and trials on these green technologies in relation to Australian plant species and climatic conditions, and promotes bushtops and living walls through publications, speaking engagements and student mentoring, in addition to their ongoing design practice.

FORM*ium* Pty Ltd, Mark McWha Landscape Architects, is an established landscape architectural practice combining professional skills in landscape design, site planning, open space, environmental planning, streetscape and urban design. The company is committed to providing innovative, high quality design solutions, balanced within the framework of real construction management and cost control constraints. The practice is known for its excellent graphic skills, and its site responsive and creative designs, which have been recognised with numerous professional state, national and international awards.

The strength of our skills and experience is best demonstrated by the broad range of successful built projects, both small scale and major works, together with a large number of repeat commissions for valued clients, in both the private and public sector.

The practice is based in Melbourne. We undertake projects throughout Australia, South East Asia, China and Japan and have an established affiliate practice in Shanghai. Major projects have been undertaken in Shanghai, Beijing, Chengdu, Tokyo, Taiwan and Brunei.

Green & Dale Associates, Landscape Architects and Environmental Planners are known for excellence in landscape architecture and its interpretation of natural and cultural places. Green & Dale Associates have developed a strong, competitive landscape architecture and environmental planning practice in Australia with expertise in a number of specialised areas. These include zoo masterplanning and design of animal exhibits, recreation facilities such as parks and botanical gardens, site planning for residential and commercial developments, and environmental studies for both natural systems and man-made projects.

The Practice's unique expertise in environmental design and planning has created an exciting 'niche' in the design of zoological and botanic gardens. With zoological gardens and theme facilities, the objective is to evoke an all-abiding love for animals, which will lead to a desire to learn about the natural world. By placing visitors into the animal's world, we intend to connect them emotionally to that world and encourage them to take an active role in supporting conservation of that world.

Imaginative design has been applied to the design of facilities such as the new Habitat Design and Interpretation for the Alice Springs Desert Park, winner of the AILA 1998 National Awards for Open Space; Masterplanning and Design for Jurong Bird Park Singapore; the African Tropical Rainforest and Gorilla Exhibit at the Melbourne Zoo, a recipient of the Australian Institute of the Landscape Architects 1992 National Award for Design; the Trail of the Elephant Exhibit at Melbourne Zoo, with its innovative interpretive storyline; and Taronga Zoo's Asian Rainforest and Australian Coastline Precincts.

The Practice provides design of outstanding quality, one based on a high level of experience and skill under the strong leadership of Green and Dale's Principal Designers.

These skills are represented in a range of areas like landscape design and planning, urban design, management plans for parklands and national reserves, interpretation and educational facilities, site analysis and visual assessment, and planning for natural / cultural resource protection.

HASSELL

Beijing
15F, Block A, TianYuanGang Center, Bing No 2, North Road of East Third Ring Road, ChaoYang District, Beijing 10027, PR China
T: +86 10 5126 6908   F: +86 10 8441 7266   beijing@hassell.com.cn

Hong Kong
Unit A, 22 / F Manu Life Tower, 169 Electric Rd, North Point, Hong Kong
T: +852 2552 9098   F: +852 2580 1339   hongkong@hassell.com.hk

Shanghai
The People's Daily Building, Level 2, 777 Century Avenue, Pudong, Shanghai 200120, PR China
T: +86 21 6887 8777   F: +86 21 5840 6281   shanghai@hassell.com.cn

Chongqing
Unit 2, 28F, International Trade Centre, No 38 Qing Nian Road, Yu Zhong District, Chongqing 400010, PR China
T: +86 23 6310 6888   F: +86 23 6310 6007   chongqing@hassell.com.cn

Bangkok
18/F K Tower, 209 Sukhumvit Soi 21, Klongtoey-Nua Wattana, Bangkok 10110, Thailand
T: +66 2207 8999   F: +66 2207 8998   bangkok@hassell.co.th

Adelaide
Level 5, 70 Hindmarsh Square, Adelaide, South Australia, 5000, Australia
T: +61 8 8203 5222   F: +61 8 8203 5200   adelaide@hassell.com.au

Brisbane
Level 3, 120 Edward Street, Brisbane, Queensland, 4000, Australia
T: +61 7 3017 5757   F: +61 7 3017 5777   brisbane@hassell.com.au

Darwin
Level 3, 59 Smith Street, Darwin, Northern Territory, 0800, Australia
T: +61 8 8981 6565   F: +61 8 8981 6561   darwin@hassell.com.au

Melbourne
61 Little Collins Street, Melbourne, Victoria, 3000, Australia
T: +61 3 8102 3000   F: +61 3 9654 1422   melbourne@hassell.com.au

Perth
Podium Level, Central Park, 152-158 St Georges Terrace, Perth, Western Australia, 6000, Australia
T: +61 8 6477 6000   F: +61 8 9322 2330   perth@hassell.com.au

Bunbury
15 Wittenoom Street, Bunbury, Western Australia, 6230, Australia
T: +61 8 9721 6700   F: +61 8 9721 6492   bunbury@hassell.com.au

Sydney
Level 2, 88 Cumberland Street, Sydney, New South Wales, 2000, Australia
T: +61 2 9273 2300   F: +61 2 9273 2345   sydney@hassell.com.au

ICN Design International
11-2-6 Jalan 3/109F, Danau Desa Business Centre, Taman Desa, 58100 Kuala Lumpur, Malaysia
T: +603 7980-3272   F: +603 7980-9504
julien@icn-design.com
www.icn-design.com
Julien Hodson-Walker

HASSELL is a design based practice with Australian origins.

HASSELL's business is planning and design and their mission is to create exceptional places for communities. HASSELL bring imagination and intelligence to projects because their work is thoughtful, process consultative, and outcomes design led yet commercially based.

Projects at HASSELL often begin with master planning when their urban designers, planners and landscape architects collaborate on project design, whilst seeking to integrate architecture and interior design into a seamless whole. The principles of sustainability underpin all projects.

Through the integrated application of these disciplines HASSELL is able to consistently add significant value to its clients' developments, particularly in the areas of health, education, urban and mixed-use development, transport infrastructure, commercial office buildings and workplace interiors.

HASSELL is owned by its Principals, has been in business since 1938, and has offices throughout Australia, in the PR of China, Hong Kong and Thailand.

ICN is a leading, award winning, Asian based consultancy operating out of Singapore and Malaysia. Our regional experience extends as far North and Beijing, through the Middle East as far as Morocco and as far South as Jakarta.

ICN goes beyond the conventional interpretation of "landscape" to offer our clients "Integrated Environmental Design". Our Principal Directors have been designing and implementing projects in Asia for more than 25 years.

Our core skills and expertise focus on Masterplanning, Hotels, Clubs & Resorts, High End Residential, Civic and Urban and Park & Recreation Landscapes.

Isthmus Group Ltd.

Auckland
43 Sale Street, Freemans Bay, PO Box 90366, Auckland,
New Zealand
T: +64 9 3099 442   F: +64 9 3099 060
akl@isthmus.co.nz
www.isthmus.co.nz
Peter Wilson

Tauranga
5 Wharf Street, PO Box 13338, Tauranga, New Zealand
T: +64 7 579 0487   F: +64 7 579 0485
tga@isthmus.co.nz

Wellington
Level 2, 49-53 Courtenay Place, PO Box 24116, Wellington,
New Zealand
T: +64 4 4999 832   F: +64 4 4999 831
wgn@isthmus.co.nz

Christchurch
Level 1, 281 High Street, PO Box 22 331 High Street, Christchurch,
New Zealand
T: +64 3 374 9937   F: +64 3 374 9938
chch@isthmus.co.nz

Jeremy Ferrier Landscape Architects
Suite 4, 72 Vulture Street, West end, 4101, Brisbane Qld., Australia
T: +61 7 3844 0700   F: +61 7 3844 0722
jjferrier@optusnet.com.au
www.jeremyferrier.com.au
Jeremy Ferrier

mcgregor+partners
P. O. Box 1083, Manly, New South Wales, Australia 1655
T: +61 2-9977-3853   F: +61 2-9976-5501
sydney@mcgregorpartners.com.au
www.mcgregorpartners.com.au
Rupert Carmichael. Associate

Isthmus Group is a nationwide New Zealand-owned company of landscape architects and urban designers working in landscape design, urban design and environmental planning.

We are a design-focused team with studios in Auckland, Tauranga, Wellington and Christchurch. Established in 1988, the company is led by 3 founding directors and currently employs 50 people.

Our vision is to provide significant improvements to a wide range of environments - Designing New Zealand to be a better place by:
- working with others inclusively as a team
- focusing on outdoor space
- fostering experts and specialists
- being leading designers
- encouraging cultural richness

We work with local government, private sector clients and collaborate with community and cultural groups, artists, planners and engineers to constantly increase the quality and richness of the process.

BACKGROUND
Jeremy Ferrier Landscape Architects is a dynamic firm of talented Landscape Architects committed to ensuring that every project we are involved with is enthused with a design flair for which we have become renowned.

We have a low boredom threshold. Churn them out, mass produced landscape designs are not our style. The success of the business has been our ability to come up with individual & fresh designs, pushing boundaries where we can & always searching for the best design solution.

This approach has led over a period of more than 20 years to the creation of landscapes of enduring quality & style. Our work has won numerous awards, is regularly published in industry journals & lifestyle magazines & is used as a resource material for lecturing in landscape design.

Director
Jeremy Ferrier BA. GDLA, AAILA, is a qualified Landscape Architect with over 23 years experience. The last 20 years has been spent as the principle of Jeremy Ferrier Landscape Architects Pty Ltd. During this time he has personally overseen the design, documentation and contract administration of a diverse range of projects covering almost all areas of Landscape Architecture. Jeremy's design flair is underpinned by an enthusiastic and talented team of young designers.

mcgregor+partners were established in 1998 with the specific aim of pursuing design innovation founded on environmental, social and economic principles. Our services cross the traditional boundaries of urbanism, landscape, culture, planning and the natural sciences to achieve innovative solutions that create value for our clients' projects.

The design studio is directed by internationally experienced senior landscape architects and urban designers who are supported by a talented and committed team working in a collaborative environment. Since studying together in Canberra in the 1980's, partners Adrian McGregor and Philip Coxall have worked on projects located across Australia, Canada, Hong Kong, Philippines, Taiwan, The United Kingdom and China.

The firm has award winning experience working in a diverse range of natural and built environments in the Australasian region and has completed over 120 projects. We regularly collaborate with other firms and disciplines either as lead consultant or as a design team member.

The firm has been published in numerous Australian, European and Asian journals and awarded prizes in three prestigious international design competitions including winning the Parramatta Road and Green Square Town Centre projects and receiving merit for the 530ha Hellenikon park competition in Athens. The Former BP Park project in North Sydney has recently won five awards including the prestigious state award for excellence in landscape architecture in NSW. Supporting our design services are efficient project management skills which have been demonstrated across a wide selection of project scales ranging from whole city regions to fine grain site designs.

Morgan+Pollard Associates Queenstown
PO Box 1269, Queenstown, New Zealand
T: +64 3 442 3448   F: +64 3 442 3449
office@greenbelt.co.nz
Ralf Krüger

Place Design Group
www.placedesigngroup.com

Brisbane
Level 1, 282 Wickham Street, Fortitude Valley, Qld. 4006 Australia
T: +61 7-3852-3922   F: +61 7-3852-4766

Sydney
Level 1, 235 Pacific Highway, North Sydney, NSW 2060 Australia
T: +61 2-9959-5021   F: +61 2-9959-5802

Gold Coast
Level 1, 8 Short Street, Southport, Qld. 4215 Australia
T: +61 7-5591-1229   F: +61 7-5591-5825

Sunshine Coast
3 / 132 Bulcock Street Caloundra Qld. 4551 Australia
T: +61 7-5499-6188   F: +61 7-5499-6711

Townsville
46 Ross River Road, Mundingburra, Qld, 4812 Australia
T: +61 7-4725-7843   F: +61 7-4725-5247

Shenzhen
10th Floor, Unit H Shen Mao Building, Xin Wen Road, Fin Tian District, Shenzhen 518026 China
T: +86 755-8294-9028   F: +86 755-8294-9438

Shanghai
Room 501 - 504, Zhongxing Trade Building, 2020 North Zhongshan Rd, Putou District, Shanghai, China
T: +86 21-5290-1155   F: +86 21-5291-0520

Fiji
Office 3A, Port Denarau Marina Village, Denarau Island, NADI Fiji
T: +679 9444-561   F: +61 7 3852-4766

UAE
Dubai Airport Free Zone Building 5EA - #620
P.O.Box 214866, Dubai, UAE
T: + 971 4-609-1650   F: + 971 4-609-1655

---

mcgregor+partners have a proven record of delivering work that meets and exceeds regulatory requirements. We regularly work with Federal, State and Local agencies, both locally and internationally, on complex projects to gain outcomes of mutual benefit to the client, community and approval authorities. We have wide-ranging experience and consultation skills to nurture projects through complex planning legislation in a judicious manner. Many of our projects have successfully gained FSA bonuses for high quality design.

mcgregor+partners project process integrates our company design approach and environmental policies with the client brief to develop the best possible options and outcomes. This is a collaborative process involving workshops with the client and consultants. We have collaborated extensively as both the lead and sub consultant with professional disciplines such as architecture; structural, civil, geotechnical, hydraulic, traffic and acoustic engineering; quantity surveyors; graphic designers; heritage consultants; community consultants and public art consultants. We work closely with these professions in a rigorous and uncompromising process to achieve imaginative and diverse outcomes.

Morgan+Pollard Associates Queenstown offers a complete range of services - landscape and environmental planning, landscape design, site planning, urban design, residential and commercial landscape design, landscape assessments, resource consent applications, project management, contract administration, community planning as well as landscape conservation (heritage and ecological). We are able to offer a range of associated services such as architecture, surveying, engineering and planning through well-established relationships with reputable companies. Morgan+Pollard Associates Queenstown has been engaged as consultants and designers throughout New Zealand.

The company has prepared landscape designs on all scales - residential site design, commercial site design, subdivision, urban design, heritage restoration, ecological restoration. Amongst the many successful examples (larger scale) are the Arrowtown Business District Upgrade Stages I, II, III and IV; Matakauri Lodge; Price, Flacks, Edgar Gardens; the Wakatipu High School Development Plan, Threepwood Ecological Restoration Plan and the Marine Parade Landscape Restoration. Presently the company works on a number of high profile urban apartment complexes, several urban residential projects, the new Frankton Marina, further stages of the Arrowtown Business District Upgrade, the Gibbston Downs Winery,several rural subdivision and residential designs. We are also involved in a number of pending Environment Court cases.

Morgan+Pollard Associates Queenstown has established itself not only as one of the primary practices in the Queenstown Lakes District but has gained significant reputation throughout the country and is now at the leading edge of the profession in New Zealand.

We also offer a comprehensive landscape contracting and landscape management service through our associated company GreenBelt Ltd.

PLACE Design Group is a dynamic multi-disciplinary consultancy with a reputation for delivering quality, sustainable, and practical outcomes for its clients. A fresh and innovative approach to each project has seen PLACE become a leader in the Planning, Design and Environment sectors of the development industry, with an ever-increasing presence in major international markets.

Rush \ Wright Associates
Level 4, 105 Queen Street, Melbourne, VIC
Australia 3000
T: +61 9600 4255   F: +61 9600 4266
inbox@rushwright.com
www.rushwright.com

Sheils Flynn Ltd
9, Leinster Avenue, London SW14 7JW, UK
T: +44 (0) 20 8876 5024   F: +44 (0) 20 8876 6627
london@sheilsflynn.com
norfolk@sheilsflynn.com
www.sheilsflynn.com
Kate Collins

Thomas Balsley Associates
31 West 27th Street, 9th Floor, New York, NY 10001, USA
T: +1 212-684-9230   F: +1 212-684-9232
info@tbany.com
www.tbany.com

Rush \ Wright Associates is an award winning design practice based in Melbourne, Australia, offering consultancy services in landscape architecture, urban design and constructed ecology. Bringing together the extensive experience and design expertise of its two founding partners, Catherine Rush and Michael Wright, the partnership has built its reputation on commitment to client service and innovative design outcomes.

Each partner has extensive experience working with private and public sector client authorities, as well as Federal, State, and Local Government bodies in the design evolution and delivery of landscape and urban design projects at the complete range of scales.

As a practice, we offer a unique combination of services, focussed on marrying client expectations with the best possible design solutions and environmental principles. We have a demonstrated track-record in designing landscapes and urban design proposals that go beyond superficial formal gestures to embrace sustainability, community values and the new environmental agenda. These are vital issues for our time.

Sheils Flynn is a collaboration, combining the talent and enthusiasm of three landscape architects, Eoghan Sheils, Stephen Flynn and Kate Collins. We take a 'hands-on' approach, with the vast majority of the work undertaken personally by the directors.

Sheils Flynn provides landscape and urban design services for cities, market towns and villages in the UK and overseas. We create high quality, meaningful landscapes which are appropriate and valued by their inhabitants and which celebrate the local spirit of a place. Our experience covers a wide and diverse range of designed spaces, including new urban squares, riverside parks, landscape restoration schemes and revitalised streetscapes. In each project the design solution draws on the character of local landscapes and cultural traditions in the surrounding hinterland.

With over 30 years of urban design experience, Thomas Balsley Associates has earned a reputation for creating environments that enhance, enrich and stimulate the individuals and communities that use them. Central to the firm's design approach is Thomas Balsley's belief that, "Public open spaces are the great democratic spaces, the ultimate common ground."

TBA's portfolio includes award-winning projects of virtually every scope and type—from urban spaces, community master plans, multi-family residences, resort communities, corporate facilities, and waterfront parks to terraces, gardens and private homes.

Among the firm's most noted commissions are Skyline Park in Denver, Gantry Plaza State Park in Queens, the Detroit Riverfront Vision Plan, South Waterfront Greenway in Portland, Chelsea Waterside Park and Riverside Park South in Manhattan, Gate City in Tokyo, and World Trade Centers in New York and Osaka. In New York City alone, Thomas Balsley has designed more than 100 public spaces, including one named in his honor, Balsley Park.

Today, the firm is considered a pacesetter in the field of urban landscape design, with an international reputation for developing environments that are creative yet responsive to their surroundings and community. The firm combines the latest in technology with personal service to clients. Extensive experience with the intricacies of the design review process ensures that concepts become completed landscapes.

Tract Consultants Pty Ltd.
195 Lennox Street, Richmond Victoria 3121, Melbourne, Australia
T: +61 3 9429 6133   F: +61 3 9429 5925
melbourne@tract.net.au
www.tract.net.au

Suite 1, Level 1, 186 Blues Point Road, McMahon's Point Sydney,
New South Wales 2060, Australia
T: +61 2 9954 3733   F: +61 2 9954 3825
sydney@tract.net.au

Level 4, 262 Adelaide Street, Brisbane Queensland 4000, Australia
T: +61 7 3229 7444   F: +61 7 3229 7400
brisbane@tract.net.au

Wraight + Associates Ltd.
PO Box 19212, 2/282 Wakefield St, Wellington,
Aotearoa New Zealand
T: +64 4 381 3355   F: +64 4 381 3366
office@waal.co.nz
www.waal.co.nz
Megan Wraight

The emergence of Tract Consultants in 1972 as Australia's first national planning, urban design and landscape design practice coincided with an unprecedented period of development in Australia.

During this thirty-year span, Australian cities were rebuilt from inside out.

In outer suburbs, new housing estates mushroomed. In old inner suburbs, modest workers' cottages were rejuvenated as desirable residences. Blighted industrial precincts were resurrected. New apartment towers rose in city centres to be inhabited by baby boomers leading the shift out of the suburbs.

Freeways, shopping centres, office towers, cemeteries, schools, universities and new public spaces were constructed or modernised There were also new wineries, resorts, casinos, conference centres, industrial estates, car parks, retirement villages, golf courses and parks.

Tract, by virtue of the breadth of its integrated planning and landscape design skills, and also its national presence in Australia's largest four cities, participated in this building boom to the extent that most Australians now come into contact with Tract's work on a daily basis. Tract's story is of a leading contemporary planning and design practice built on uniting two professional disciplines that developed in isolation from each other for over half a century: planning and landscape design.

Wraight + Associates Ltd, established in 2003 was formerly Megan Wraight Landscape Architects established in 1998. As a result of the projects completed by Wraight + Associates Limited, this company has an established reputation in the areas of Landscape and Urban Design.

As Landscape Architects, Wraight + Associates are particularly interested in the way cultural, historical and natural processes interact to shape the landscape. We design environmental infrastructure in both public and private landscapes. Furthermore, we believe in the multi-disciplinary approach to ensure that the final built product is responsive to, and reflective of the complex interelationship and systems that define urban environments.

Landscape Design